Chuck and Blanche J[

M000102882

Savor™
Denver
and the Front Range
Cookbook

with Tracy Johnson

Wilderness Adventures Press, Inc.
Belgrade, Montana

This book was manufactured with an easy-open, lay-flat binding.

© 2004 by Chuck and Blanche Johnson
Photographs contained herein © 2004 as noted

Map, book design, and cover design © 2004 Wilderness Adventures Press, Inc.™

Published by Wilderness Adventures Press, Inc.™
45 Buckskin Road
Belgrade, MT 59714
1-800-925-3339
Web site: www.wildadv.com
E-mail: books@wildadvpress.com
First Edition

Chuck and Blanche Johnson's Savor™ Cookbook Series
All rights reserved, including the right to reproduce this book or portions thereof in any form or by any means, electronic or mechanical, including photocopying, recording, or by any information storage and retrieval system, without permission in writing from the publisher. All inquiries should be addressed to: Wilderness Adventures Press, Inc.™, 45 Buckskin Road, Belgrade, MT 59714

Printed in the United States of America

Library of Congress Cataloging-in-Publication Data

Johnsons, Chuck.
  Savor Denver and the Front Range cookbook / Chuck & Blanche Johnsons.
    p. cm.
  ISBN 1-932098-09-7
  1. Cookery, American. 2. Cookery–Colorado. I. Johnsons, Blanche. II. Title.
  TX715.J625 2004
  641.5973–dc22

                                        2004016910

ISBN 1-932098-09-7

TABLE OF CONTENTS

INTRODUCTION

The area of Denver and the Front Range is a unique combination of cosmopolitan cities with a true Western flavor, featuring a number of fine restaurants and creative chefs. The people of Denver are blessed with a profusion of first-rate dining establishments. Statistics show that the area has one of the highest per capita rates of restaurants. Many outstanding chefs who have made their name in the larger cities of our country have made the choice to practice their profession in Colorado because of the outstanding opportunities for outdoor recreation and the laid-back style of the West. In this, the third in our series of Savor Cookbooks, we are happy to present many of these restaurants.

It is important to note that all of the featured restaurants were by invitation. None of the restaurants are charged for appearing in the book. We selected them based on the excellence and uniqueness of their food, as well as their ambience. Many have interesting histories.

Our daughter, Tracy Johnson, has been a resident of Denver for ten years. Tracy selected the restaurants that appear in this book, and will be collaborating with us on the forthcoming book in the series that will feature the fine restaurants and lodges in the Colorado mountains. She also provided the great photos of the area and many of the restaurant photos, and helped us select the interesting historical photos you will find scattered throughout the book.

The reader can use this book as both a cookbook and a travel guide. Savor Denver and the Front Range has over 125 delicious recipes that you can take pleasure in recreating in your own home. The recipes and the restaurant descriptions will also give you a flavor for the type of cuisine you can expect in each of the restaurants, and the map will help you locate them. We hope you enjoy reading and using this book as much as we enjoyed putting it together.

Dog Saloon in 1898

ACKNOWLEDGMENTS

We would like to give our special thanks to the owners, managers, and chefs of the featured restaurants for their help in gathering the information in this book, as well as their generosity in sharing some of their favorite recipes with us.

Our appreciation extends to the gracious staff members of both the Colorado Historical Society and the Stephen H. Hart Library. Their voluminous files gave us a wealth of photos from which to choose.

We also want to thank Tracy's friends and colleagues in the food and beverage industry for their helpful suggestions.

Of course, this project would not have made it to fruition with out the tireless efforts of Lynn Kinnaman, our project manager and editor, and Mark Woodward, our graphic designer.

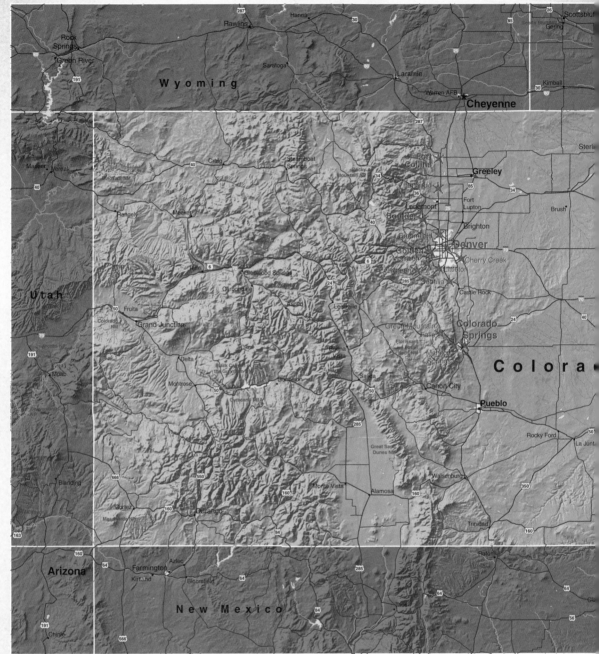

©2004 Wilderness Adventures Press, Inc.

RESTAURANT LOCATIONS

SAVOR™ DENVER
AND THE FRONT RANGE
COOKBOOK

FEATURED RESTAURANTS

Berthoud
  Savoy
Boulder
  Brasserie 1010
  Flagstaff House
  Greenbriar Inn
  Red Lion
Broomfield
  Chef Jam
Cherry Creek
  Fourth Story (Tattered Cover)
Colorado Springs
  Broadmoor Hotel
  Jake & Telly's Greek Cuisine
Denver
  1515
  Aix Restaurant
  Avenue Grill
  Barolo Grill
  Brasserie Rouge
  Buckhorn Exchange
  Celtic Tavern
  Emmas
  Painted Bench
  Restaurant Kevin Taylor
  Rocky Mountain Diner
  Samba Room
  Strings

Evergreen
  Restaurant Kody
Fort Collins
  Braddy's Downtown Restaurant
  Jay's Bistro
  Nico's Catacombs
Golden
  Briarwood
Green Mountain Falls
  Black Bear
Littleton
  Manor House
  Opus Restaurant
Manitou Springs
  Briarhurst Manor
  Cliff House at Pikes Peak
Morrison
  The Fort
Sedalia
  Gabriel's

DENVER FACTS

Date Founded: November 17, 1858
Elevation: 5,280 feet
Population (2002): 554,636
Land Area: 154.63 square miles
Largest Employment Sectors: Services, Government, Retail
Major Industries: Communications, Utilities, Transportation

Historic Landmark Designations (2003)
> **Districts:** 42
> **Structures:** 305

Denver Public Libraries (2001): 23
> **Circulation:** 12,486,851

Municipal Parks and Recreation
> **Park Area:** 5,100 acres
> **Parks:** 301
> **Golf Courses (public and private):** 15
> **Parkways:** 100 miles
> **Recreation Centers:** 29
> **Swimming Pools:** 19
> **Hike/Bikeways:** 135 miles
> **Mountain Parks:** 13,600 acres
> **Playing Fields:** 325
> **Tennis Courts:** 143

Notable Dates in Denver's History:
> 1903   First hunting licenses issued in Denver for a one dollar fee.
> 1906   First coins produced at the US Mint in Denver.
> 1914   First buffalo reintroduced back into the state of Colorado at Genesee mountain park west of Denver.

Platte River

The steps of the capital and the mile high marker.

1515

Restaurant

1515
restaurant

1515 Market Street
Denver, CO 80202
303-571-0011
www.1515restaurant.com

Monday-Friday
Lunch 11:00 am – 2:00 pm
Monday-Saturday
Dinner 5:00 pm – 10:00 pm

1515 Restaurant
Gene Tang, Owner
Olav Peterson, Chef

When you walk into 1515 Restaurant from busy Market Street, you immediately feel the difference. It's like another time, one where the world was less frantic and elegance was the norm. A long-standing Denver restaurateur, Gene Tang has created an atmosphere that makes you feel very comfortable and welcome. He takes the time for personal attention to both his guests and his restaurant. Gene genuinely cares about each diner's experience, and often makes changes based on the feedback he receives from his customers.

The restaurant has received many accolades over the years, including "Best Dinner Destination for Impressing a Date" from Westword. The restaurant has also won the "Award of Excellence" from the Wine Spectator for four years in a row.

Housed in a red brick building, circa 1860, the restaurant features high ceilings with filigreed wrought iron accenting the brick walls. Vintage photographs of downtown Denver are found throughout the establishment. A focal point is the beautiful cherry bar that was renovated and brought from St. Louis. The main dining room is upstairs and offers comfortable seating for large groups as well as intimate seating for romantic dinners.

Chef Olav Peterson creates delightful eclectic Colorado dishes with fresh local ingredients, often featuring buffalo, and Colorado lamb. He also adds his own flair to dishes from other regions, such as the Maryland blue crab cakes, served with chipotle cream and lime jam, which you can order from the appetizer menu. The smoked duck breast with golden raisin reduction and the seared sea scallops with crisp cherry polenta and grapefruit beurre blanc on the dinner menu illustrate the variety that Chef Peterson creates for the dining experience. Lunches offer more of the same great dishes, along with a truly gourmet selection of beef and buffalo burgers. The Rocky Mountain News named the Kobe burger "Best Burger 2003".

A special "Tasting Dinner" offers the opportunity to order your own wine or choose one selected especially for the food served. The wine list features more than 300 different selections, many available by the glass. There is also a wine sommelier available to help you choose the perfect accompaniment for your dinner selections.

In 1515, Gene Tang has created a special atmosphere that allows his guests to relax and enjoy a special dining experience that truly reflects the eclectic feeling of Denver.

Award of Excellence – Wine Spectator, 2001, 2002, 2003, 2004

CARAMELIZED GOAT CHEESE TERRINE
WITH GRAPEFRUIT JAM
appetizer

Ingredients

10 grapefruits, peeled and segmented
¼ cup honey
¼ cup granulated sugar
2 ounces aged goat cheese

3 ounces smoked goat cheese
4 ounces goat cheese
½ cup turbinado sugar

Preparation

IN small saucepan, combine grapefruit, honey, and sugar. Reduce the ingredients on low heat until it becomes a thick, jam-like consistency. Stir frequently to make sure jam does not scald.

ONCE reduced, remove from heat and transfer jam into a small container. Refrigerate.

LINE a chilled terrine mold with plastic wrap, leaving overlap on both sides of the mold. Crumble aged goat cheese and press the cheese into bottom of mold, up to six inches deep, making sure top is flat and level. Spread half the grapefruit jam evenly on top of the cheese layer.

CRUMBLE smoked goat cheese and press evenly on top of the layer of jam. Spread remaining grapefruit jam on top of second layer of cheese. Press the remaining goat cheese into the terrine, making sure it is level with the top of the mold.

FOLD the overhanging sides of the plastic wrap on top of the last cheese layer and firmly press down to settle all the ingredients. Chill the terrine for at least two hours.

ONCE chilled, remove from terrine mold by gently pulling on plastic wrap. Slice into ½ inch thick pieces. Just before serving dip one flat side into turbinado sugar and caramelize with a small butane torch.

Serves 6

Wine suggestion: Argyle Nut House Pinot Noir or New Zealand Noblio Icon Sauvignon Blanc

CRAB STUFFED HALIBUT
WITH VANILLA JASMINE RICE AND GRAPEFRUIT
BEURRE BLANC

Ingredients

6 8-ounce halibut filets
6 pieces large rice paper
¼ pound rinsed chives

1 pound crabmeat (claw)
Vanilla Rice (recipe follows)
Grapefruit Beurre Blanc
(recipe follows)

Preparation

BUTTERFLY halibut, leaving one side connected. Using equal portions of the crabmeat, fill the opened halibut. Once all six are stuffed, fold the connected half over, returning the piece to its original shape.

SOAK the rice paper in warm water until pliable (approximately 30 seconds). Place rice paper on a clean surface, separating all six pieces, and spread flat. Place equally portioned chives on top of rice paper. Place halibut on top of the chives. Season with salt and pepper, then wrap the halibut in the chives. Fold the rice paper on opposite ends, then fold over the bottom side and roll onto last side. Gently place halibut on a lined tray and refrigerate.

PREHEAT oven to 400 degrees. Heat a large, oven-safe sauté pan over high heat and add oil. Once oil is hot, gently place halibut pieces in pan, seam side down. Once edges of rice paper start to brown, gently flip each over, careful to not pierce the outside of the rice paper or allow rice paper to stick to pan, and place pan in oven and cook for approximately 10 minutes.

For the Vanilla Rice

1½ cups uncooked jasmine rice
1 vanilla bean

3 cups water
2 tablespoons granulated sugar

SPLIT the vanilla bean and scrape out seeds, being careful not to collect long fibrous material in the scrapings. In small saucepan, bring water to a boil. Add rice, sugar, and vanilla seeds. Stir quickly with a wire whisk and cover. Reduce heat to low and let sit for approximately 20 minutes. Remove from heat and fluff rice with a large spoon.

For the Grapefruit Beurre Blanc

1-2 *teaspoons oil*	1 *cup fresh grapefruit juice*
1 *shallot, thinly sliced*	¼ *cup honey*
1 *garlic clove, minced*	¼ *pound unsalted butter*

PLACE oil in small saucepan on medium heat. Add shallot and garlic. Sauté ingredients until translucent, and add grapefruit juice. Once the grapefruit juice begins to reduce, add honey and whisk together. Reduce to a thick, almost syrup-like, consistency. Lower heat and slowly whisk in butter until completely melted. Sauce should be thick with a smooth and even consistency.

Strain sauce through a fine sieve, discarding the leftover shallots and garlic.

Serves 6

Wine suggestion: Chateau Sourvair Chardonnay, Sonoma, California, a nice, buttery white wine.

The main dining area at 1515.

BANANA POUND CAKE

Ingredients

2 sticks butter
3 ripe bananas, peeled
½ cup cake flour
½ cup all purpose flour

1 cup chopped dark chocolate
6 large eggs
1 cup sugar

Preparation

IN A high-speed mixer, whip butter to twice its volume.

ADD bananas and sugar. Continue to whip in the mixer until ingredients are evenly combined and creamy. While whipping ingredients, slowly add eggs, one at a time, until mixture is even and smooth.

TRANSFER to a large mixing bowl and sift in both flours. Mix thoroughly. Add chocolate and blend evenly. Place in a buttered 9 /12 x 4 x 4 bread pan and bake in oven at 350 degrees for approximately 45 minutes, or until center is sturdy.

Serves 10

The Avenue Grill

630 East 17th Avenue
(17th Avenue at Washington)
Denver, Colorado 80203
303-861-2820
www.avenuegrill.com

Monday-Thursday
11:30 am - 11:00 pm
Friday-Saturday
11:30 am - 12:00 am
Sunday
5:00 pm - 10:00 pm

The Avenue Grill
Bill Ferguson, Owner
Andrew Lubatty, Executive Chef
Shelly McCandless, General Manager

Chef Andrew Lubatty.

The Avenue Grill building was constructed in 1924 with retail on the ground floor and the El Dorado apartments on the second floor. In 1986 Cliff Young renovated the restaurant space and installed the 1940's vintage bar, opening The Avenue Grill as a high end Mexican restaurant. Cliff's partner, Bill Ferguson, is the current owner and the catalyst in changing the fare from Mexican to a San Francisco style restaurant. The restaurant was purchased in 1988 and renovated to the current look with grand wood furnishings and brass fixtures giving it an elegant, sophisticated yet casual atmosphere reminiscent of the 30's and 40's. From each white linen-draped table you have a view onto the busy uptown 17th Avenue through the wall-to-wall windows.

The San Francisco style menu features food from the four sections of the city by the bay: North Beach, the Wharf, Chinatown and old San Francisco. This diversity was planned to match the diverse uptown neighborhood in which they are centered. On any given afternoon or evening, their friendly, professional staff welcomes an array of Denverites, ranging from artists to lawyers to local business people, as well as a host of out-of-town guests.

The Executive Chef, Andrew Lubatty, has been at The Avenue Grill for three years. Chef Andrew was trained at the Culinary School of America and, before coming to The Avenue, traveled for 10 years, working in many different resorts, hotels and restaurants across America. Among his many career highlights, Chef Andrew was in charge of corporate menu development and research at Berringer Vineyards in California.

Chef Andrew enjoys combining techniques from classic to modern and adds many ethnic twists. With the San Francisco theme, he has created a menu featuring Pacific Rim and Italian influences, using many West Coast seafoods and produce.

Under the professional, charming direction of General Manager Shelly McCandless, you will always feel welcome and a part of the family when dining at The Avenue.

Avenue Grill, Denver

8

The Avenue Grill's bar is a great for cocktails.

WILD MUSHROOM STRUDEL
appetizer

Ingredients

2 cups button mushrooms, sliced
2 cups shiitake mushrooms, stemmed,
   and caps sliced
1 tablespoon garlic, minced
¼ cup sliced shallots
2 tablespoons olive oil
2 tablespoons brandy
1 tablespoon fresh herbs (basil,
   tarragon or parsley)

salt and black pepper to taste
4 ounces goat cheese
¼ cup Parmesan cheese, shredded
6 sheets phyllo dough
   melted butter for dough
   organic spring greens
   Balsamic Syrup (recipe follows)
   Chive Oil (recipe follows)
   Chili Oil (recipe follows)

Preparation

HEAT a sauté pan and add olive oil, mushrooms, garlic, and shallots. Cook until softened, about four minutes. Add brandy carefully, tilting pan away from you to ignite.
Season with herbs, salt, and black pepper, then remove pan from heat.
Add cheeses and stir in until well combined, cool to room temperature.

LAY one sheet of phyllo dough on counter, and brush it with butter. Repeat two times to make three layers, then cut the sheet in half vertically down the center. Place one quarter of mixture in a 1"x 3" bar across bottom section of phyllo, roll up, tucking sides in as you get towards the top. Repeat with other three strudels. Brush outside of strudel with additional butter, place on cookie sheet and bake at 375 degrees for 15-20 minutes or until golden brown. Remove from oven and let cool for five minutes.

TO SERVE, place a mound of greens on center of plate. Slice strudel diagonally in half and rest against greens. Drizzle with balsamic syrup, chive, and chili oils.

For the Chili Oil

½ cup olive oil
2 teaspoons chili powder
2 teaspoons water

ADD water to chili powder and mix to make paste, stir into olive oil and strain.

For the Chive Oil

   2 *tablespoons chives, sliced*
   ½ *cup olive oil*

PUREE chives with oil in food processor, and strain.

For the Balsamic Syrup

   ½ *cup balsamic vinegar*

PLACE balsamic vinegar in non-reactive saucepan and simmer until reduced in volume by half.

Serves 4

SESAME SEARED AHI TUNA

Ingredients

   4 *7-ounce pieces of Hawaiian ahi tuna*
   ¼ *cup mixed black and white sesame*
      seeds
      kosher salt and pepper
      vegetable oil to sear
      Ponzu Butter (recipe follows)
      Wasabi Potatoes (recipe follows)

Asian vegetables (broccoli, cooked carrots, daikon, snow peas, red bell pepper, etc.)
sesame oil to taste
soy sauce to taste
lemon, quartered
pickled ginger (optional)

Preparation

SEASON ahi with salt and pepper to taste, remembering that the sauce will be slightly salty from the soy sauce. Roll in sesame seeds.
Heat pan and add oil, searing on all sides for 30 seconds per side for rare, 1 minute per side for medium rare or finish on lower heat for more well done.
Place on wasabi potatoes and Asian vegetables seasoned with a splash of sesame oil and light soy. Garnish tuna with ponzu butter, lemon and pickled ginger.

For Ponzu Butter

1 teaspoon sesame oil	¼ cup light soy sauce
1 tablespoon minced ginger root	2 pieces star anise
1 tablespoon shallot, sliced	½ cup heavy cream
½ cup white wine, such as Chablis or Chardonnay	1 stick butter (4 ounces)

HEAT sesame oil in non-reactive saucepan and cook ginger and shallot for 30 seconds. Add wine, soy sauce, and star anise. Simmer until mostly evaporated. Add cream and simmer until evaporated and thickened. Add butter in slices and stir well to blend in smoothly. Strain and keep slightly warm until needed.

For Wasabi Potatoes

wasabi to taste
mashed potatoes for four

ADD prepared wasabi (equal parts of powder and water) to mashed potatoes, adjusting amount of wasabi to desired intensity; potatoes should have a slight green color.

Serves 4

View of the dining area and bar inside the Avenue Grill.

CHINATOWN PORK CHOP

This marinade works well on salmon, mahi mahi, swordfish, shrimp, or a good steak! Just make sure you cook it in a pan to make a nice glaze on the outside.

Ingredients

4 pork rib chops, frenched bones, rib bone only
Hoisin Marinade (recipe follows)
2-4 tablespoons vegetable oil

wasabi to taste
mashed potatoes for four
¼ cup chicken broth
pickled ginger (optional)

Preparation

POUND chops between two sheets of plastic wrap to ½ inch thickness, place chops in hoisin marinade for a minimum of 15 minutes, up to a maximum of 8 hours.

WHEN ready to cook, heat sauté pan, add a little vegetable oil and cook chops until well browned, flip and place in 400 degree oven until desired doneness.

ADD prepared wasabi (equal parts of powder and water) to mashed potatoes, adjusting amount of wasabi to desired intensity. Potatoes should have a slight green color.

PLACE potatoes in center of plate and rest chop against potatoes, add a little chicken broth or water to pan, swirl to mix and place a little on chop, this is a light sauce.

FINISH with pickled ginger on top. A vegetable egg roll or your favorite vegetable goes well placed next to the potatoes.

For the Hoisin Marinade

½ cup soy sauce
1 tablespoon sesame oil
1 tablespoon garlic chili paste
⅓ cup hoisin sauce
½ cup honey

1 tablespoon Szechwan peppercorns, toasted
2 teaspoons garlic, minced
¼ cup Dijon mustard
3 tablespoons cilantro, chopped
2 tablespoons fresh ginger, minced

COMBINE in bowl and use as needed.

Serves 4

JACK DANIEL'S CHOCOLATE BREAD PUDDING

Ingredients

4 egg yolks
⅓ cup sugar
½ cup milk
2 cups cream
4 ounces semi-sweet chocolate, melted

¼ cup Jack Daniel's whiskey
3-4 each egg burger buns, diced
    Streusel Topping (recipe follows)
    ice cream and caramel sauce
    (optional)

Preparation

COMBINE egg yolks and sugar in bowl. Bring milk and cream to a boil. Remove from stove and slowly whisk hot cream into egg and sugar mixture. Return mixture to stove, and cook over medium heat, stirring constantly until slightly thickened. Remove from heat and add melted chocolate, stirring well.

ADD whiskey and burger buns and soak for 15 minutes. Pour into buttered molds. Sprinkle streusel topping mixture liberally over puddings before baking.

BAKE at 350 degrees until set, about 25-30 minutes. Finish with vanilla ice cream and caramel sauce.

For the Streusel Topping

1 stick butter, diced into ¼ inch chunks
¼ cup sugar
¼ cup brown sugar
1 cup flour

3 tablespoon cocoa powder
¾ teaspoon cinnamon
¼ teaspoon salt

COMBINE topping ingredients in mixer bowl, using paddle attachment. Run slowly until mixture becomes crumbly.

Serves 4

THE WINE SPECTATOR AWARD

Many of the restaurants included in this cookbook have been recognized by Wine Spectator, the world's most popular wine magazine. It reviews more than 10,000 wines each year and covers travel, fine dining and the lifestyle of wine for novices and connoisseurs alike. Through its Restaurant Awards program, the magazine recognizes restaurants around the world that offer distinguished wine lists.

Awards are given in three tiers. In 2003, more than 3,600 restaurants earned wine list awards. To qualify, wine lists must provide vintages and appellations for all selections. The overall presentation and appearance of the list are also important. Once past these initial requirements, lists are then judged for one of three awards: the Award of Excellence, the Best of Award of Excellence, and the Grand Award.

- Award of Excellence—The basic Award of Excellence recognizes restaurants with lists that offer a well-chosen selection of quality producers, along with a thematic match to the menu in both price and style.
- Best of Award of Excellence—The second-tier Best of Award of Excellence was created to give special recognition to those restaurants that exceed the requirements of the basic category. These lists must display vintage depth, including vertical offerings of several top wines, as well as excellent breadth from major wine growing regions.
- Grand Award—The highest award, the Grand Award, is given to those restaurants that show an uncompromising, passionate devotion to quality. These lists show serious depth of mature vintages, outstanding breadth in their vertical offerings, excellent harmony with the menu, and superior organization and presentation. In 2003, only 89 restaurants held Wine Spectator Grand Awards.

 Award of Excellence    Best of Award of Excellence

 Grand Award

Barolo Grill

3030 East 6th Avenue
Denver, Colorado 80206-4328
303-393-1040

Tuesday-Saturday
5:30 pm - 10:30 pm
Closed Sundays and Mondays

Barolo Grill

Barolo mezzanine.

E leven years ago restaurateur Blair Taylor spent a summer in Italy's Northwestern Piedmont region. Upon his return, he decided to open a new restaurant, hoping to bring the foods and wines of Piedmont to Denver, Colorado. He decided to name it "Barolo Grill," after Piedmont's most famous wine.

The idea and concept of Barolo Grill has always been to try and recreate the experience one would have in a restaurant in northern Italy. In order to assure this authenticity, Mr. Taylor has taken all the employees of this restaurant with him to northern Italy every summer. The staff has the unique opportunity to visit wineries, meet with the wine makers, and taste the cuisine of Piedmont, Tuscany, and the Veneto. This assures that the chef's recipes are as authentic as possible, as well as providing new ideas for the menu. For the wait staff and management, it assures that they can knowledgeably explain the food and wine of northern Italy to the patrons of Barolo Grill.

The restaurant is designed to look and feel like a Tuscan farmhouse, the sort of "rustic elegance" that Italy thrives on and Barolo Grill recreates wonderfully. The wine list is ranked among the best in the country. Over 800 different wines are featured, with many selections from Italy, especially Barolo, Barbaresco and Brunello. The menu changes frequently, with the dishes always remaining true to the foods of the northern Italian regions of Piedmont, Tuscany, and the Veneto. Everything is made in-house, fresh daily - the pasta, the gelato, and the bread. Nothing is bought pre-made. This continuously highlights the authenticity, much like most restaurants in Italy.

A warm cheerful mood exudes from the restaurant, much of which is created by Mr. Taylor, who is at the restaurant nearly every night, greeting guests, making sure everyone is comfortable. He is up front on the pride he takes from fine dining.

"A quality meal with beautiful wine stops the frantic pace of life and slows you down enough to put the world in perspective," he says. "The dinner table with food and wine accomplishes so much. It grounds you, cheers you, and lets you catch your breath. Good wine and food are the most magical of pairings."

 Best of Award of Excellence

BEET SALAD

Ingredients

6 beets – 3 red and 3 golden
2 cups walnuts
1 cup Gorgonzola cheese
1 cup champagne vinegar

½ cup + 1 tablespoon olive oil
   salt and pepper to taste
   handful of greens (lolorosa or red oak)
1 bunch of asparagus, grilled

Preparation

ROAST beets in a heavy pot, skin on, for 3-4 minutes. Set aside, cool and slice. Toast walnuts in oven until lightly browned.

IN A bowl, mix Gorgonzola, vinegar, and ½ cup olive oil until creamy. Add salt and pepper.

IN A sauté pan, warm beets, asparagus, walnuts, and remaining olive oil. Then add dressing and a handful of greens and serve.

Serves 6

LAMB OSSO BUCO

Ingredients

4 lamb shanks
1½ cups flour
1 tablespoon coriander powder
1 tablespoon salt
1 tablespoon pepper
1-4 tablespoons olive oil
3 carrots, diced

3 red onions, diced
1 cup celery, chopped
4 cups white wine
3 cups San Marzano tomatoes
1 quart stock, either veal, chicken, lamb
   or vegetable

Preparation

Bread lamb shanks with mixture of flour, coriander, salt, and pepper. Brown in heavy saucepot with olive oil. Remove from heat, let pot cool. Add chopped vegetables to shanks, heat, add wine and reduce by one third. Add tomatoes and stock, bake in oven at 350 degrees for 2 ½ hours.

Serves 4

SMOKED DUCK RIBOLLITA

Ingredients

2 celery stalks
1 large onion
2 carrots, peeled
10 cloves garlic
¼ cup olive oil
½ cup Marsala wine
1 sprig rosemary
10 sage leaves
2 sprigs thyme

4 cups duck stock
1 cup cooked white beans
  salt and pepper to taste
  dried focaccia croutons
1 smoked duck breast
10 arugula leaves, chiffonade
¼ cup shaved Parmigiano-Reggiano
  cheese
  extra virgin olive oil

Preparation

CHOP celery, onion, carrots, and garlic. Sauté in olive oil until tender. Add Marsala, reduce to half the original volume.

ADD herbs and duck stock. Bring to boil until vegetables are tender. Reduce heat; add beans and season with salt and pepper.

PUT a layer of croutons in a serving container, ladle soup over. Repeat layering process until soup is used up. Cool and refrigerate.

TO SERVE, reheat soup and garnish with sliced duck breast, arugula leaves, cheese, and extra virgin olive oil.

Serves 6–8

17th Street from Union Station, Denver. (1906-1910)

Brasserie Rouge

1801 Wynkoop St.
Suite 150
Denver, CO 80202
303-991-2242
www.brasserierouge.com

Sunday and Monday
5 pm - 10 pm
Tuesday - Thursday
5 pm – 10:30 pm
Friday and Saturday
5 pm – 11 pm

Brasserie Rouge

Brasserie is derived from the French word for "brewer" and originated in the northern part of France. Brasseries were originally country establishments that served beer and substantial portions of hearty food. Many brasseries were based on the regional food of Alsace, an area fought over by France and Germany, but over time they came to offer more wine than beer and a varied menu including Fruits de Mer (literally, "fruits of the sea") a cold seafood platter that contain the freshest of the day's delivery and bistro specialties such as leg of lamb, steak au poivre and steak tartare.

Brasseries also differed from the typical Parisian establishment by offering continuous menu service well into the night. Evoking a true brasserie, Brasserie Rouge is casual, but stylish, a restaurant that is open for late night dining, offering anything from an omelet and a glass of wine to oysters, vegetarian selections or crepes. All the menu selections at Brasserie Rouge – from pastries and desserts, to stocks and sauces, as well as the entrees and hors d'oeuvres – are made in-house, fresh every day, and are served within an atmosphere that replicates the true warmth, bustle and casual chic-ness of the original French brasseries. And, of course, the traditional warm baguette is brought to your table in white paper while you peruse the menu, deciding between the Coq au Vin or the Rabbit a' la Moutarde.

Due to the importance that the French tradition places on food and wine pairings, Brasserie Rouge strives to provide a list of wines that can be enjoyed on their own or easily paired with the varied food menu. With a current list of over 200 wines, ranging from a Grand Cru to Vin de Table, Brasserie Rouge has a wine selection that acknowledges new wines from around the world, while still drawing heavily from French producers.

The restaurant is located in lower downtown Denver, in the historical Icehouse building, and the interior takes you away from the outside elements. The glowing brass, dark wood, backlit marble bar, antique alabaster lamp and the twenty-foot glass enclosed wine cabinet are reflected in the mirrors and establish the French character. The service is warm and friendly, whether you are rushing to a game or play or you are simply enjoying time with your friends.

The dining room at Brasserie Rouge.

Coq au Vin

Ingredients

4 skin-on chicken breasts, cut in half
1 cup oil
   salt and pepper to taste
   flour for dredging
1 tablespoon fresh sage or marjoram
   leaves
2 cups Pinot Noir
1 pound bacon, thinly sliced and baked
   until lightly colored

2 pints red pearl onions, blanched, and
   peeled
1 pound quartered button mushrooms,
   sautéed until colored, and seasoned
4 teaspoons unsalted butter
2 tablespoons chopped parsley
   sherry vinegar
   Chicken Braise (recipe follows)
   Saffron Couscous (recipe follows)

Preparation

THE night before, begin by preparing the chicken braise, following the recipe below. The day of, preheat oven to 400 degrees.

IN A few large straight-sided sauté pans, heat the oil. Salt and pepper the chicken breasts, dredge in flour, and brown slowly on both sides. Drain off the excess oil and add the marjoram or sage. Add the Pinot Noir, reduce by half, and add the chicken braise. Bring to a simmer, cover the pans, and place in the oven for 10 minutes. Prepare the saffron couscous.

REMOVE the chicken pieces with a slotted spoon to plate and cover with foil. Reduce the liquid by half. Heat the bacon in the oven. Add the pearl onions and button mushrooms and swirl in the butter. Add parsley and a few drops of sherry vinegar.

TO SERVE, pour the ragout over the chicken and serve with warm saffron couscous.

For the Chicken Braise

8 chicken legs
8 chicken thighs
1 cup kosher salt
4 tablespoons ground black pepper
1 tablespoon cayenne pepper
2 tablespoons ground cumin
2 tablespoons paprika
   flour for dredging
2 cups neutral oil

3 large carrots, peeled and cut on the
   bias
3 onions, sliced
6 cloves garlic, sliced
   salt
   pepper
3 tablespoons tomato paste
1 bottle Pinot Noir
3 quarts chicken stock
2 bay leaves

THE night before, heat some of the oil almost to smoking in a few large straight-sided pans. Mix the salt, black pepper, cayenne pepper, cumin, and paprika together and season the chicken legs and thighs generously with the mixture, dredge in flour and shake off the excess. In batches, slowly brown the chicken in sides, then transfer to a baking pan. Wipe out the pans, add fresh oil, and slowly cook the carrots and onion until softened. Add the garlic, salt, and pepper and cook until the garlic is fragrant. Add the tomato paste and cook 2 minutes, stirring often. Add the red wine, bring to a full boil, and add the chicken stock and bay leaf. Bring to a boil again, skim well, and pour the liquid over the chicken pieces. Preheat oven to 325 degrees.

COVER the chicken with the foil and bake for about 90 minutes, or until the chicken easily comes off the bone. Remove the chicken pieces, carrots, and onions to a plate, and chill, covered. Strain the cooking liquid and degrease thoroughly. Cool and pour over the chicken. Refrigerate until needed.

For the Saffron Couscous

2 teaspoons extra virgin olive oil	6 cups water
2 teaspoons butter	salt
2 yellow onions, diced fine	freshly ground black pepper
1 teaspoon minced garlic	pinch cayenne pepper
6 cups couscous	pinch saffron
6 cups chicken stock	2 bay leaves

IN A 2-gallon heavy-bottomed pot, heat oil and butter, and cook onions until tender but not colored, about 10 minutes. Add garlic and cook until fragrant but not colored. Add couscous and toss well to coat. Add stock, water, salt, pepper, cayenne, saffron, and bay leaves. Bring to a boil, then turn to down a low simmer and cover. Cook 8-10 minutes and turn out onto a sheet tray. Fluff with two forks, adjust seasonings, and hold in a bain-marie lined with a damp cloth.

Serves 8

CASSOULET

Ingredients

6 pork shanks
salt
black pepper
canola oil for cooking
1 large carrot, thickly sliced
1 large yellow onion, sliced
4 cloves garlic, sliced
2 tablespoons tomato paste
1 quart white wine
6 quarts chicken stock
3 bay leaves
3 branches rosemary

4 cups bread crumbs
2 tablespoons butter
2 cups diced bacon
3 cups diced onions
2 cups diced celery root
2 cups diced butternut squash
2 cups diced carrots
2 tablespoons minced garlic
2 tablespoons minced rosemary
3 cups Pinot Noir
    White Beans (recipe follows)

Preparation

THE night before, season the shanks with salt and pepper and refrigerate. Soak the white beans, according to recipe below.

THE following day, heat the canola oil in a large pot and brown the shanks on all sides. Heat the oven to 300 degrees.

WIPE out the pan, add fresh oil, and cook the carrot. Add onion and cook until slightly colored and softened, about 10 minutes. Add the garlic and cook until fragrant but not colored. Add the tomato paste and fry about 2 minutes. Add the white wine and reduce by half. Add the chicken stock, bay leaves, and rosemary, bring to a boil and pour the liquid over the shanks. Cover with foil and cook in the oven for about 4 hours, until the meat comes off the bone. Remove the shanks, skim the cooking liquid, and strain it into a bowl set in ice. Degrease completely. Shred the meat off the shanks, check for seasoning and return it to the cooking liquid.

HEAT the braising liquid and the beans together. Simmer gently and, after 10 minutes, add ¼ of the bread crumbs. Add another ¼ of the bread crumbs every 10 minutes, until the bread crumbs are gone and the beans are thick but not dry.

IN another pan, heat the butter, add the bacon, and cook until tender and lightly colored. Add the onions, celery root, butternut squash, and carrots and cook until tender and lightly colored. Add the garlic and rosemary and cook until fragrant. Add the red wine and reduce by two-thirds. Add this mixture to the beans and cook 10 minutes. Cool and adjust the seasoning.

For the White Beans

4 cups dried cannellini beans
12 cups cold water
8 cups chicken stock
2 teaspoons kosher salt
2 bay leaves
12 cloves garlic

THE night before, soak the white beans in cold water. The next day, drain the beans well, and place in a pressure cooker with the remaining ingredients, and cover. Heat to the second notch on the cooker. Cook for 10 minutes, then rinse the cooker under cold water for 12 minutes, and drain the beans.

Serves 20

Brasserie Rouge's wine room.

Hazelnut Shortbread Sandwich
with Fig Compote, Haystack Mountain Chèvre and Fig Syrup

Ingredients

1 cup blanched, toasted hazelnuts
¼ cup cornstarch
1⅔ cup flour
1 teaspoon salt
1 teaspoon ground black pepper
1 teaspoon fresh thyme leaves

¾ cup soft butter
½ cup sugar
3 egg yolks
fig syrup
Whipped Goat Cheese (recipe follows)
Fig Compote (recipe follows)

Preparation

PREHEAT oven to 325 degrees. In a food processor, coarsely grind hazelnuts. Add cornstarch, flour, salt, pepper, thyme, and pulse until fine. Set aside.

IN A mixer with the paddle attachment, whip the butter and sugar until light. Add the egg yolks. Add the dry ingredients, and mix just until combined.

CHILL 1 hour. Pat the dough between two sheets of floured parchment. Roll to ¼" thickness.

CUT dough into cookies, using a 1¼" pastry cutter. Place on several sheet trays lined with parchment paper.

BAKE 8-10 minutes until lightly golden along the edges. Cool.

TO ASSEMBLE, use the pastry bag to pipe a little of the goat cheese mixture on a hazelnut cookie. Top with a circle of fig compote, then a little more goat cheese. Top that with a cookie. Plate with a small pool of fig syrup.

For the Whipped Goat Cheese

2 pounds fresh goat cheese, room
   temperature
3 cups heavy cream

1 teaspoon salt
½ teaspoon ground black pepper

IN A mixer with a paddle, whip the goat cheese 2-3 minutes. Add the cream, pulse, and whip the mixture with salt and pepper until smooth, transfer to a pastry bag with a round tip.

Hazelnut Shortbread Sandwich
with Fig Compote, Haystack Mountain Chèvre and Fig Syrup
CONTINUED

For the Fig Compote

5 pounds Calymrna figs, stem end and
  bottom removed, sliced ⅓" thick
2 bottles Pinot Noir
3 cups sugar
1 tablespoon roasted cracked black
  pepper

2 tablespoons toasted fennel seeds
  pinch of salt
  few drops balsamic vinegar

IN A one-gallon non-reactive pot, whisk together the Pinot Noir and sugar until dissolved. Bring to a simmer, add the figs, and cover with a round of parchment paper. Simmer about 45 minutes over very low heat until the figs are very tender and the syrup is thick. Add the pepper, fennel, pinch of salt and a few drops of balsamic vinegar. Strain the cooking liquid through a chinois and reserve. Chill the compote.

Makes about 160 cookies

Main dining area.

Buckhorn Exchange

1000 Osage St.
Denver, CO 80204
303-534-9505
www.buckhorn.com

Lunch - Monday - Friday
11 am - 2 pm
Dinner - Monday - Thursday
5:30 - 9 pm
Friday and Saturday
5:00 pm – 10:00 pm
Sunday
5:00 pm – 9:00 pm

The Buckhorn Exchange
Bill Dutton, General Manager

The Buckhorn Exchange was established by Henry H. "Shorty Scout" Zietz in 1893. Zietz, a true Old West character, joined Col. "Buffalo Bill" Cody at the tender age of 12 and became part of his hard-riding, straight-shooting band of scouts. From the very beginning, the Buckhorn Exchange drew cattlemen, miners, silver barons and railroad men, the movers and shakers of the fledgling western frontier.

The name comes from the Rio Grande Railroad yards, located across Osage Street, and the Buckhorn Lodge, the second-story motel. At the end of every week, railroaders rushed to the exchange to trade their paychecks for gold. Zietz, a shrewd businessman, gave each one a token for free lunch and a beer.

Prohibition put many such establishments out of business, but Zietz simply went with the flow. He converted the front of the restaurant and saloon into a grocery store. When Prohibition was repealed, the restaurant/bar reopened and today proudly displays Colorado Liquor License No. 1, purchased for $35 in 1935.

The Buckhorn Exchange is full of historical artifacts, photos, and western memorabilia, including 500 taxidermy pieces. The 125-piece gun collection includes Colt .45's, Winchesters, derringers, a Sharp's sporting rifle from 1889, and a rare palm pistol from the 1890's. Photos on display have been autographed by Bob Hope, James Cagney, Roy Rogers, Will Rogers, Ronald Reagan, Jimmy Carter, and Dwight D. Eisenhower. The building is on the National Register of Historic Places and was designated as a historic landmark by the city and county of Denver in 1972.

The Buckhorn Exchange features food based on authentic ingredients, indigenous to the Old West. Meat such as buffalo, elk, pheasant, and other game that Buffalo Bill Cody and Teddy Roosevelt hunted appear on the menu, accented with chiles, dried fruits, spring onions, roasted red pepper and juniper berries. Appetizers include alligator tail, rattlesnake, smoked buffalo sausage, and Rocky Mountain Oysters.

The Old West influence joins Henry Zietz's German and Pennsylvania Dutch culinary heritage, in a setting reminiscent of yesteryear, making the Buckhorn a true experience for all the senses.

ROCKY MOUNTAIN OYSTERS
appetizer

Some folks may get squeamish about the thought of actually preparing these gems from the southside of a bull, so better to just come in and enjoy ours. But for the adventurous, here's how to prepare them.

Ingredients

10 bull testicles
 1 cup plain bread crumbs

½ cup all purpose flour
   salt and pepper to taste

Preparation

FOR breading, combine bread crumbs and flour, add salt and pepper to taste. The bull testicles must be partially frozen, so they are easier to peel. Cut the testicle in half and pull the skin off. Slice them about ¼ of an inch thick and bread them.

DEEP fry the slices until golden brown, about 4-5 minutes. Serve with cocktail sauce or horseradish cream sauce.

Serves 6

Buffalo Red Eye Stew

Ingredients

- 2 pounds buffalo stew meat (preferably sirloin)
- 4 potatoes, peeled and cut in 1 inch cubes
- ¼ pound butter
- ½ yellow onion, chopped
- ¼ tablespoon white pepper
- ¼ tablespoon leaf thyme
- ¼ tablespoon whole rosemary
- ½ tablespoon basil
- ½ tablespoon salt
- 1½ tablespoons granulated garlic
- 1 cup flour
- 1 28-ounce can diced tomatoes
- ½ cup bourbon
- ½ cup strong coffee
- 1 tablespoon Worcestershire
- 2 cups water

Preparation

PLACE potato cubes in saucepan, cover with water, and bring to boil. Reduce heat to simmer and continue to cook until potatoes are about half done. While potatoes are simmering, melt butter in a large saucepan over medium heat; add stew meat, onions and dry spices. Simmer while potatoes are cooking. When potatoes are about half done, add flour to pan with buffalo and mix well. Cook for 5 minutes.

ADD the can of tomatoes and stir into the buffalo mixture. Let simmer for 5 minutes. Drain potatoes and add the balance of ingredients; gently stirring together. Return to a boil, reduce heat and allow to simmer for half an hour or until buffalo is tender. Serve in a large hollowed out loaf of sheepherder's bread.

Serves 2-4

Prime Rib of Buffalo
with Seven Seed Crust

Ingredients

6-7 pounds buffalo prime rib
      olive oil to coat
  1   tablespoon anise seeds
  1   tablespoon whole coriander
  1   tablespoon fennel seeds
  1   tablespoon mustard seeds

  1   tablespoon celery seeds
  1   tablespoon Tellicherry peppercorns
  1   tablespoon green peppercorns
  1   teaspoon sea salt
  1   cup beef stock
  1   cup good cabernet

Preparation

ONE day prior to cooking, remove the roast from refrigerator. Trim all exterior fat to 1/8 of an inch and tie between the rib bones in order for roast to hold its flavor.

RUB exterior of the rib with a small amount of olive oil until evenly coated.

PLACE the seven seeds and salt in a blender or spice grinder and process until the consistency of coarse corn meal.

EVENLY coat the roast with the spice blend and return to refrigerator for about 24 hours.

WHEN ready to cook, preheat the oven to 425 degrees. Place the roast in a shallow pan and place in the oven for 20-30 minutes until the seeds are roasted to a deep brown. Reduce the oven temperature to 325 degrees and continue to cook until the meat reaches an internal temperature of 120 degrees.

REMOVE from the oven and let stand for 15 minutes. Remove the roast from pan and place on a cutting board and cover with foil and a kitchen towel.

POUR the pan drippings through a mesh strainer, filled with lots of ice, into a small saucepan (this will remove the excess grease). Place the saucepan on the stove and add the beef stock. Add the cabernet and bring to a boil, reduce to a simmer.

REMOVE the rack of bones and slice into servings of desired thickness or number. Serve with au jus.

Serves 8-12

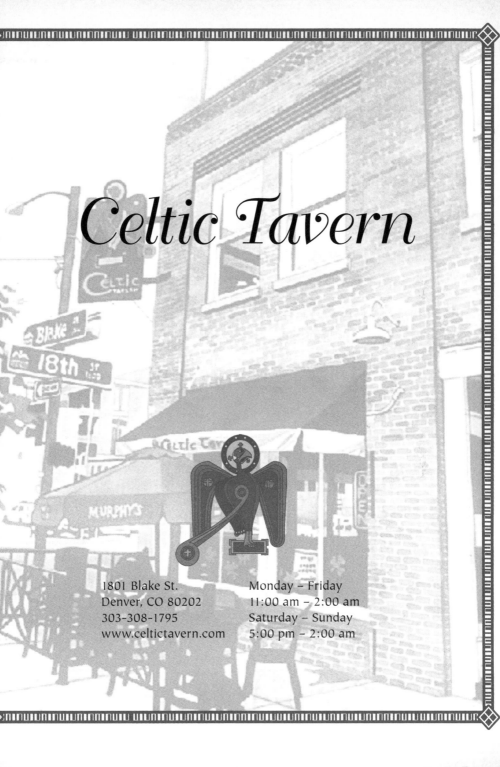

Celtic Tavern

1801 Blake St.
Denver, CO 80202
303-308-1795
www.celtictavern.com

Monday – Friday
11:00 am – 2:00 am
Saturday – Sunday
5:00 pm – 2:00 am

Celtic Tavern

Terry Brennan, John Higgins, Noel Hickey, and Patrick Schaetzle, Owners

The Celtic Tavern is one of the most popular taverns in LoDo. Noel, John, and Patrick, (three of the four owners - the fourth lives in Ireland), welcome you with enthusiasm and warm hospitality. Always ready with a funny joke, the three will entertain you with their dry Celtic wit.

The Celts were an ancient people of northwestern Europe who at one time, over 2000 years ago, lived all over Britain, Ireland, France and parts of Spain and Germany. Their culture was rich in art, music, and poetry.

The Celtic Tavern represents the Welsh-Irish-Scottish heritage. It's a true Celtic pub. The walls are decorated with hundreds of antique books, historical quotes, and Celtic signs. The extensive list of imported beers, whiskeys, and cigars reflects the rich history of the three countries and the menu ranges from typical Irish/English fare to more intricate dishes like seafood casserole.

Everything in the Celtic Tavern is genuine, handmade and much of it has been brought over from Ireland. The bar is one of the longest in the area, and the 150-year-old stained glass behind it is from a Dublin hotel. The mahogany table in the Robert Burns room came from the Irish Parliamentary Hall.

The restaurant's wrap-around front and side windows offer a view to the busy downtown streets. In the evenings, the bar is jumping. If you are looking for a quiet corner, you can't go wrong in the Robert Burns Room, where you can have a cigar or just enjoy the rich wood, leather sofas, and fireplace with a friend. Downstairs you can sip on your single malt scotch while getting an old-fashioned shoeshine.

SCOTCH EGGS
with Scotch Whiskey Sauce

In the "old country" these tasty treats used to be made up the night before and put into the lunch sacks of miners. Now school children take the eggs on school outings for a snack. We have added our own Scotch whiskey sauce to the presentation and serve the eggs right out of the oven.

Ingredients

- 2 tablespoons Coleman's mustard powder
- ½ teaspoon whole caraway seed
- ¼ teaspoon ground allspice
- ½ teaspoon granulated garlic
- ½ teaspoon granulated onion
- ¼ teaspoon black pepper
- pinch salt

- ½ pound ground pork sausage
- ¼ pound ground beef
- ¼ pound ground chicken breast
- 2 eggs, lightly beaten
- 6 hard-boiled eggs (shelled)
- bread crumbs
- Scotch Whiskey Sauce (recipe follows)

Preparation

MIX first 11 ingredients well. Mixture should be moist. Divide evenly into 6 portions. Coat each hard-boiled egg with mixture and roll in breadcrumbs. Bake in a 350 degree oven for 30 minutes.

EGGS may be served warm or cold, with Scotch Whiskey Sauce.

For the Scotch Whiskey Sauce

- ½ cup honey mustard dressing
- 1 tablespoon Dijon mustard
- 1 tablespoon whole grain mustard

- pinch fresh dill
- 1 ounce scotch whiskey

TO MAKE sauce, blend honey mustard dressing, Dijon mustard, whole grain mustard, fresh dill and scotch whiskey well and chill.

Serves 6 as an appetizer or 3 as a main course

A nice measure of Oban Scotch Whiskey will wash these eggs down.

POTATO & LEEK SOUP

An Irish classic! Served with some Irish soda bread or potato bread, this is a meal in itself.

Ingredients

¾ pound bacon, chopped
 5 chopped leeks, white portion only
½ gallon beef broth
¼ pound potatoes, diced

1¼ pounds mashed potatoes
 1 tablespoon oregano
 1 teaspoon garlic, chopped
 1 teaspoon black pepper

Preparation

SAUTÉ bacon until just cooked, not crispy, add leeks, and cook until they just turn limp. Add broth, potatoes, and spices. Simmer for 30 minutes or until diced potatoes are done.

Serves 10–20

A pint of Murphy's Red beer will go nicely with this piping hot bowl of soup. Or when you visit the Tavern, try our famous and exclusive house beer "Max Evans", a Welsh style lager.

COD FISH CAKES

Light and flaky cod blended with onions, herbs, egg and bread crumbs. A great lunch entrée or dinner appetizer.

Ingredients

1 pound cod filet, chopped
½ large onion, finely chopped
1 egg beaten
½ teaspoon thyme, chopped
⅓ cup bread crumbs
¼ teaspoon salt

½ teaspoon pepper
1 tablespoon parsley, chopped
oil for cooking
mixed greens and lemon wedges for garnish

Preparation

MIX cod filet, onion, egg, thyme, salt, pepper, parsley and ¼ cup of the bread crumbs together. Set aside the remainder of bread crumbs for dusting. Divide into four portions and form into patties. Dust each cake lightly with bread crumbs. Sauté lightly in oil until brown. Finish in a 350 degree oven for 8 minutes or until cooked through. Serve with mixed greens and fresh lemon wedges.

Makes 4–5 cakes

Try a pint of Stella Artois, a light Belgian beer, with these great fish cakes.

STEAK AND MURPHY'S PIE

This is one of our most popular dishes, made with real Irish beer. Serve piping hot with a small salad on the side.

Ingredients

5 pounds cubed beef (stew meat)
1 quart Murphy's Irish Stout (or any good quality stout beer)
1 teaspoon chopped garlic
3 bay leaves
1 teaspoon black pepper
4 tablespoons beef base

2 medium onions, diced
6 medium carrots, diced
2 tablespoons corn starch, dissolved in ½ cup of cold water
2 sheets of pastry dough (frozen pastry dough will need to be thawed)

Preparation

PRE-HEAT oven to 350 degrees. Combine beef, beer, garlic, spices and beef base in a large ovenproof stew pot and cook in oven for 30 minutes. Add onions and cook for an additional 20 minutes. Then add carrots and cook for an additional 15 minutes or until carrots are tender. Total oven cooking time is approximately 65 minutes. Remove from oven and thicken with cornstarch. Divide stew into six 8-ounce casserole dishes and top with pastry dough. Return to oven and bake until pastry dough is golden brown, about 15 minutes.

Serves 6

To be enjoyed with a cold pint of Murphy's Irish Stout, of course.

CELTIC TAVERN IRISH CREAM BREAD PUDDING

Ingredients

1 loaf stale French bread	1¼ cups sugar
2 cups milk	1 teaspoon vanilla
1 cup heavy cream	½ cup raisins
½ cup St. Brendan's Irish Cream	Caramel Irish Cream Sauce
2 tablespoons unsalted butter	(recipe follows)
3 eggs	

Preparation

CRUMBLE the bread, complete with crust, into a mixing bowl. Cover with milk, cream, and St. Brendan's Irish Cream. Let mixture stand until the bread has absorbed most of the liquid (approximately 45 minutes).

PREHEAT oven to 325 degrees, butter a 13" X 9" baking dish and set aside.

BEAT eggs, sugar, and vanilla until they are well blended. Mix gently with the bread mixture and raisins. Spoon into a baking dish and smooth out top, so it is even. Bake until light brown and custard is set (approximately one hour).

For the Caramel Irish Cream Sauce

¼ cup water	⅓ cup heavy cream
1 cup sugar	1 teaspoon lemon juice
⅓ cup freshly brewed coffee	¼ cup St. Brendan's Irish Cream

MIX sugar and water in a saucepan. Cook until the mixture turns a nut brown, stirring often. Remove from heat. Handling carefully, to avoid splatter, immediately pour coffee and heavy cream into saucepan. Return to heat and cook, stirring constantly until caramel melts. Remove from heat and cool. Stir in lemon juice first, then St. Brendan's Irish Cream, mix thoroughly. Serve over sliced bread pudding.

Serves 8

Larimer Street Denver, Colorado. Teams of oxen pull wagons. (between 1862 and 1864)

Emma's Restaurant

603 East 6th Avenue
Denver, CO 80203
720-377-3662
www.emmasrestaurant.com

Tuesday –Saturday
5:00 pm –10:00 pm

Emma's

This small little restaurant on the corner of Pearl and 6th is perfect for a romantic dinner for two. Garren and Linda Austin have a combined total of 45 years in the restaurant business. They met when both were working at the Brown Palace. In fact, some of the furnishings were obtained from the Brown Palace auction.

Garren and Linda left the restaurant business in order to start a family, but the lure of the business was still in Garren's blood. That's when Linda decided to help him start his own restaurant, named after their young daughter. The space is small and intimate, with three separate dining rooms featuring overstuffed chairs, soft lighting and colorful paintings by local artists. The hand-decorated salt and pepper shakers were created by Emma.

Garren knows the importance of a professional wait staff, and you will enjoy the prompt and efficient service that you will receive. The staff takes care to make sure you are served at the pace that you desire, without feeling rushed. Along with a smoke-free policy, the restaurant also insists on no cell phone usage, which contributes to the relaxed atmosphere.

When first opened, Emma's served more of a twist on home-style, comfort food. With new chef, Brian Sack, the menu has been taken up a notch with unique flavors, though still staying dedicated to Emma's philosophy of classic cuisine. Brian is a graduate of the Broadmoor Hotel's Culinary Internship Program, and is the former Executive Chef at The Tattered Cover's Fourth Story.

One of his signature appetizers is the smoked wild boar paté atop toasted pistachio brioche and drizzled with a port chipotle reduction. For entrees, try the applewood smoked

buffalo short ribs atop toasted cumin seed mashed potatoes with a charred tomato and hatch green chili salsa. Or the seafood lover will enjoy the fresh diver scallops, lemon risotto, and spicy ginger coconut milk and lemongrass sauce.

Emma's was voted the "Most Romantic Restaurant - 2004" by the Rocky Mountain News.

BABY RED AND GREEN ROMAINE SALAD
with Cracked Black Pepper Port Vinaigrette
and Toasted Walnuts and Lemon Stilton Cheese

Ingredients

16 ounces port wine	salt and pepper
1 tablespoon black pepper	water
1 shallot, minced	baby green and red romaine for two
1 tablespoon Dijon mustard	servings
¼ cup red wine vinegar	4 ounces lemon Stilton
1 cup oil	⅛ cup walnuts, toasted

Preparation

REDUCE port wine and black pepper by three-fourths and cool. Combine shallot, Dijon, red wine vinegar, and port wine/pepper reduction in bowl. Add oil, whisking slowly. If vinaigrette seems thick, lighten up with water, as desired. Season with salt and pepper.

TO MAKE one serving, fan red romaine on bottom of plate, then fan baby green romaine on top, keeping both lettuces visible. Ladle one ounce of vinaigrette over the greens. Finally, place a two ounce piece of lemon Stilton and some of your toasted walnuts on top and enjoy. Lemon Stilton is an English dessert cheese that can be found in most cheese shops or gourmet markets.

Serves 2

SWEET POTATO AND GINGER SOUP
with Whipped Cardamom Cream

Ingredients

½ yellow onion, diced
1 carrot, peeled and diced
1 tablespoon fresh ginger, diced
1 tablespoon butter
2 cloves garlic, minced
½ teaspoon nutmeg
2 sweet potatoes, peeled and diced
2 cups heavy cream

2 quarts chicken or vegetable stock (red miso)
1 bay leaf
salt and pepper to taste
Whipped Cardamom Cream (recipe follows)
fresh mint

Preparation

START by sweating the onion, carrot, and ginger with butter in a medium saucepan on medium high heat for eight minutes. Add garlic, nutmeg, and potatoes, and sauté for two more minutes. If necessary, add more butter or oil. Then add the heavy cream, stock, and bay leaf and cook on low heat until potatoes are tender. Puree all ingredients in a blender. If puree looks too thick, add more stock or cream to desired thinness, strain through a medium fine mesh strainer, and season to taste with salt and white pepper.

TO SERVE, place serving of soup in a bowl and top with a tablespoon of whipped cardamom cream on top. Garnish with fresh mint.

For the Whipped Cardamom Cream

2 cups heavy cream
1 teaspoon ground cardamom
½ teaspoon ground cinnamon

WHIP heavy cream, ground cardamom and ground cinnamon until stiff peaks form.

Serves 4-6

CURRIED GREEN LENTILS WITH A HAZELNUT TUILE
and Goat Cheese Packages

Ingredients

4 cups French green lentils (soak overnight)
1½ quarts vegetable stock or chicken stock
1 bay leaf
1 teaspoon salt
ham hock (optional)
1-2 tablespoons oil or butter
1 red onion, medium dice
½ tablespoon garlic, minced

1 tablespoon curry paste
1 teaspoon orange zest
2 tablespoons apple cider
1½ cups chicken or vegetable stock
¼ cup heavy cream
salt and pepper to taste
1 bunch chopped cilantro
Hazelnut Tuile (recipe follows)
Goat Cheese Packages (recipe follows)

Preparation

IN A medium saucepan, place lentils, stock, bay leaf, salt, and ham hock, cook for 10 minutes or until lentils are tender. Strain and set aside.

TO SERVE, heat oil or butter in a large sauté pan on high heat. Cook red onions, garlic, and curry paste for five minutes. Turn heat down to a low simmer and add lentils, orange zest, apple cider, stock, cream, and any meat remaining on ham hocks. Salt and pepper to taste. Finally, place in an ovenproof dish and bake for 20 minutes at 300 degrees.

TO SERVE, place one cup of cook lentils in center of plate. Then place hazelnut tuile, and put cooked goat cheese package on top. Enjoy!

For the Hazelnut Tuile

¼ pound butter
1 cup powdered sugar
4 egg whites

1 cup flour
½ cup hazelnuts, chopped fine
1 teaspoon vanilla extract

CREAM butter and sugar. Slowly add egg whites, flour, and hazelnuts. Add extract. Spoon 1-2 tablespoons of batter on a non-stick cookie sheet (a silicone baking mat works well), leaving room to spread. If you like, cut in a design shape. Cook in a 350 degree oven for 8 to 10 minutes.

CURRIED GREEN LENTILS WITH A HAZELNUT TUILE
and Goat Cheese Packages
CONTINUED

For the Goat Cheese Packages

> 1 eggplant
> olive oil
> 8 ounces goat cheese
> Salt and pepper to taste

SLICE eggplant lengthwise very thin, a little less than a ¼ inch. Lightly coat eggplant with some olive oil and grill on one side for four minutes. Remove and let cool. Roll goat cheese in a cylindrical manner two inches in diameter and freeze for eight minutes, or until you can get a clean 2-inch slice. Finally, wrap goat cheese with one slice of eggplant, folding the sides first, like a burrito. Salt and pepper to taste. To cook, place packages on a greased sheet pan and broil for 5-6 minutes.

Serves 4-6

ELK RACK WITH JUNIPER BERRY GLAZE
Candied Crab Apples and Pumpkin Garlic Potato Puree

While you can cook the elk any way you desire, this recipe is designed for the avid grill person. This recipe can be changed from elk rack to tenderloin or leg, depending on the number of guests.

Ingredients

> 1 cinnamon stick
> 1 bottle of Merlot wine (2 quarts), preferably Plum Creek or Palisade Colorado
> 1 vanilla bean, split lengthwise
> 1 teaspoon whole black peppercorns
> 2 bay leaves
> 3 whole cloves
> 1 tablespoon whole juniper berries

> 2 whole cloves fresh garlic, crushed
> 1 fresh sprig rosemary
> 1 elk rack (8 bones per rack)
> Juniper Berry Glaze (recipe follows)
> Pumpkin Potatoes (recipe follows)
> Candied Crab Apples (recipe follows)
> fresh flat leaf parsley
> fresh raspberries

Preparation

PLACE first nine ingredients in a large saucepot and bring to a boil. Simmer for 10 minutes. Cool to room temperature. Then place elk rack in and marinate for a minimum of one day, or a maximum of four days. The longer, the better!

COOK the meat and prepare the glaze, potatoes, and crab apples. To serve, place a scoop of pumpkin potatoes in the center of plate. Then place elk up against the potato so that the elk is using potato to prop itself up. Ladle one ounce of sauce over the elk. Finally, place candied apple on plate, decorate with sprigs of flat leaf parsley and fresh raspberries.

For the Juniper Berry Glaze

1 tablespoon canola oil or vegetable oil
2 cloves garlic, crushed
2 teaspoons whole juniper berries
2 cups balsamic vinegar

1 cup veal stock or beef broth
1 tablespoon butter
salt
pepper

HEAT canola or vegetable oil in small saucepan on medium heat. Add garlic and juniper berries. Saute for 30 seconds, or until garlic is slightly hazelnut in color. Then add balsamic vinegar and reduce by half. Finally, add your veal stock or beef broth and simmer on low heat for 5 minutes. Finish the sauce by stirring in your butter and season with salt and pepper.

For the Pumpkin Potatoes

3 whole russet potatoes, peeled and
    diced ½ inch thick
2 cloves fresh garlic, crushed
    water to cover
1 8-ounce can pumpkin puree
1 cup heavy cream

1 cup butter
1 tablespoon fresh parsley, chopped
½ teaspoon nutmeg
    salt
    white pepper

BOIL potatoes and garlic in salted boiling water. Use only enough water to cover the potatoes. When potatoes are soft, place in a medium bowl with remaining ingredients. Whip to desired consistency.

For the Candied Crab Apples

6 medium crab apples
12 ounces granulated sugar
1 cup water

ELK RACK WITH JUNIPER BERRY GLAZE
Candied Crab Apples and Pumpkin Garlic Potato Puree
CONTINUED

CUT the bottom off crab apples so that the flat side of the apple sits down. Place a piece of waxed paper on a large baking sheet pan. Place apples on the baking sheet in rows of three, giving the apples space. In a medium saucepan, heat sugar and water on high heat. Once the sugar comes to a boil, do not stir. At this point you want to brush sides of the pot with a brush dipped in a little water to keep the sugar from crystallizing. When your sugar becomes a light brown, turn heat off and set aside. Now take a large spoon and spoon a good amount of the sugar over the apples in a straight line. You want individual lines for each apple. Cool ten minutes.

Serves 4

Elitch's Garden, theater entrance, Denver, Colorado. (between 1900 and 1910)

Painted Bench

400 E 20th Ave
Denver, CO 80205
303-863-7473
www.paintedbenchdenver.com

Monday – Friday
11:00am - 11:00 pm
Saturday
5:00 pm - 11:00 pm

The Painted Bench
Bill and Steve Rohs, Owners

Bill and Steve in doorway.

Named for the brightly colored bench painted by kids at the Children's Hospital, Painted Bench is a classic neighborhood bistro owned by brothers Bill and Steve Rohs. The restaurant is located across from a park and is part of the newly upgraded downtown neighborhood with many new businesses and condominiums. The old historic building adds a special charm having served as a drug store for many years.

In 1999, the brothers started renovating the building themselves. In replacing the floor, they found and removed a total of two layers of carpet and ten layers of linoleum. They have kept the original drug store soda fountain in the Fountain Room, and use it as the bar. The historic pictures on the wall are of interest to anyone curious about Denver's history. One of the original tenants, John F Coulson, served many a delicious soda fountain treat from this bar. The brothers have named a signature drink after him, the John F. Coulson Prescription Manhattan. The brothers created the drink after finding an old whiskey bottle during renovations.

The Rohs celebrate their fifth anniversary with the Painted Bench in 2004. Their restaurant offers a comfortable home feeling with a variety of furniture and bookshelves filled with books, pictures and knick-knacks.

Bill and Steve Rohs share a love of innovative food and it shows in their menus. The appetizer menu offer many tempting items, including an antipasto with duck paté, aged Gorgonzola, Haystack Mountain goat cheese, shaved prosciutto, Cabernet poached pear, aged pecorino cheese, and honey. For pasta, try the Wild Mushroom and Leek Ravioli served with a sherry and white wine cream sauce with lavender and honey spaghetti squash. The Pan Seared Ahi Tuna is sure to please served with seafood avocado wontons, steamed baby bok choy and a lobster and roasted yellow pepper puree. The lunch menu is equally enticing with thick sandwiches, burgers (including elk), salads and pastas.

Mark Drug doorway, 1945.

ASPARAGUS SALAD WITH OLIVES AND CAPERS

Ingredients

3 bunches asparagus, blanched
¼ cup capers

Mushroom Vinaigrette (recipe follows)
Marinated Kalamata Olives
(recipe follows)

Preparation

PREPARE the marinated Kalamata olives and mushroom vinaigrette.

TO ASSEMBLE the salad, put the asparagus in a bowl and add enough mushroom vinaigrette in the bowl to cover the asparagus with a nice coating. Season with salt.

TAKE 8-10 asparagus stalks on a plate, with all the heads facing the same direction, put 4-6 olives on the plate, along with equal amounts of capers and enjoy.

For the Mushroom Vinaigrette

1 portobello mushroom
¼ cup extra virgin olive oil
1 shallot, diced

REMOVE the fans from the portobello mushroom and dice. Put a tablespoon of olive oil in a sauté pan, over medium high heat, add the diced mushroom and shallot, and cook for ten minutes until mushroom is soft. Put the mushroom and shallot mix in a blender and add the rest of the olive oil, blend together.

For the Marinated Kalamata Olives

¼ cup Kalamata olives
   olive oil to cover
1 sprig rosemary

1 sprig thyme
2 teaspoons cardamom

PUT the olives in a shallow saucepan and add enough olive oil to cover, then add the sprig of rosemary, the sprig of thyme and the cardamom. Heat over low heat and let the olives simmer for about 20 minutes, then let them rest for about two hours. Remove the rosemary and the thyme.

Serves 4-8

Painted Bench, Denver

Sea Scallops and Ricotta Salata Gnocchi and Sautéed Rapini

With Sauce American

Ingredients

20 large sea scallops
1 tablespoon salt
5 tablespoons butter
3 tablespoons olive oil
  one bunch rapini, blanched

4 Roma tomatoes, peeled, seeded, and chopped
  Ricotta Salata Gnocchi (recipe follows)
  Sauce American (recipe follows)

Preparation

SALT one side of the scallops. Put 3 tablespoons butter and 2 tablespoons olive oil in the pan, add the scallops, sauté on each side for about two minutes, then set aside in warm place. Prepare the gnocchi and the sauce American, according to the directions below.

BRING a pan of salted water to a boil, add the gnocchi, and simmer until they rise to the top, about one minute. In a saucepan, heat the remaining 2 tablespoons butter and 1 tablespoon olive oil over medium heat. Strain the gnocchi and put them in the saucepan with the butter and olive oil, and sauté for about one minute. Add the rapini and sauté for about one minute more, then add the tomatoes and sauté until warm, approximately 30 seconds.

TO SERVE, arrange some of the gnocchi and rapini in a bowl, put 5 sea scallops on top of the gnocchi and ladle enough sauce American in the bowl to cover the bottom.

For the Ricotta Salata Gnocchi

2 Idaho potatoes
1 tablespoon salt
2 egg yolks
1 bunch fresh chives

2¼ cups all purpose flour
⅛ cup ricotta salata cheese (broken into very fine pieces)

BOIL the potatoes until they are fork tender, strain well. Put potatoes through the ricer while still warm (smashing the potatoes will not work, they must go through the ricer). Cool the potatoes to room temperature, and add salt, egg yolks, and chives. Add flour, incorporating it into the potatoes by kneading, as you would a simple bread dough. Along with the last bit of flour, add the ricotta salata cheese.

THE dough should be moist, but not stick to your hands. Divide the dough into six pieces and roll into long, ¼ inch round strips. Using a sharp knife, cut into ½ inch pieces, transfer to a parchment lined sheet pan. Cover with dry cloth and set aside in the refrigerator.

For the Sauce American

2 tablespoons butter	½ cup brandy
1 tablespoon olive oil	1 cup lobster stock
4 shallots, peeled and diced	¼ cup heavy cream
2 cloves garlic, minced	1 sprig of tarragon
1 tablespoon tomato paste	3 tablespoons white truffle oil
½ cup white wine	2 tablespoons white wine vinegar

IN A saucepan, heat the butter and the olive oil, add the shallots, and cook for one minute. Add the garlic and tomato paste and cook for two minutes more. Deglaze with white wine and reduce by half. Add the brandy, reduce to ¾, add the lobster stock, reduce by half, add the cream and tarragon sprig and bring to a simmer. Strain, then add the truffle oil, white wine vinegar and salt. Hold in a warm area. This can be made in advance and warmed before serving.

Serves 4

Inside the Painted Bench.

ROASTED CHICKEN

Ingredients

1 whole chicken, 3-4 pounds
1½ shallots, diced
1 tablespoon olive oil
1 cup dried figs
1 cup dried apricots
1 cup dried golden raisins
½ cup sherry
½ cup white wine

2½ tablespoons soft butter
salt and pepper
1½ carrots, chopped
1 onion, chopped
½ stalk celery, chopped
juice of 1 lemon
2½ tablespoons melted butter
butcher's twine

Preparation

IN A saucepan, over high heat, add shallots and olive oil, sweat down the shallots, then add all the dried fruit, sherry, and white wine. Turn down heat to a low simmer (you do not want to allow the liquid to evaporate before the dried fruit can absorb it). Simmer until all the liquid is absorbed, about 20-25 minutes.

TAKE 1-1½ tablespoons of the soft butter and work it under the skin with your fingers, being careful you don't rip the skin as you are doing this. Season with salt and pepper. Preheat the oven to 450 degrees. Take the shallot and fruit mixture and put equal parts into the cavity of the bird. Tie the cavity of the bird shut with the butcher's twine, looping from the neck and working your way back to the cavity of the bird, tying legs together to close the opening of the bird.

IN A roasting pan, place the carrots, onions, and celery, setting the chicken on top of the vegetables. Cook the chicken for 25 minutes at 450 degrees, then turn the heat down to 350. Brush the chicken with melted butter and continue to do so every five minutes once the skin begins to brown. Brushing with lemon juice will make the skin crisp. The chicken should be done in about 50 minutes, or until the juices run clear from the leg and thigh area.

ONCE the chicken is done, remove twine and stuffing. Put stuffing in a sauté pan with the pan juices or drippings, bring to a boil, season with salt and pepper to taste and serve warm with chicken.

Serves 4

PORK TENDERLOIN
with White Bean Stew

Ingredients

2 whole pork tenderloins, with silver skin removed	¼ pound shiitake mushrooms
3 cups of white beans, soaked overnight	½ cup carrots, diced
4 quarts of water	2 shallots, diced
1 smoked ham hock	2 cloves garlic, diced
1 carrot, chopped	1 cup of chicken stock
1 onion, chopped	salt and pepper to taste
3 strips apple smoked bacon, diced, fat rendered off	butter to taste
	2 tablespoons olive oil and canola blend

Preparation

USE a stockpot large enough to hold twice the amount of liquid and beans. Put the white beans, water, ham hock, chopped carrots, and onions and simmer for 3-4 hours until tender. Be careful not to boil the beans or they will separate from each other. Once the beans are cooked, strain and reserve the liquid (bean water) and remove the ham hock.

TO MAKE the stew, use a medium stockpot and cook the bacon over medium heat for two minutes. Add the shiitake mushrooms, carrots, shallots, garlic, and cook for 15 minutes, or until the mushrooms are sweated down. Add the white beans and the chicken stock and ¼ cup of the bean water. Simmer for 25 minutes or until the liquid is reduced by two-thirds. Season with salt, pepper, and butter.

SEASON the pork tenderloin with salt and pepper. Heat a sauté pan over medium high heat, place two tablespoons of canola and olive oil blend in the pan, and sear the pork on all sides. Finish cooking in 350 degree oven to desired doneness (usually 25-30 minutes or until internal temperature is between 150° to 165°).

TO ASSEMBLE, ladle enough of the bean stew into the bowl to cover the bottom, slice the pork tenderloin and lay 3-4 slices over the beans and serve.

Serves 6-10

WARM CHOCOLATE TRUFFLE CAKE

Ingredients

- 1 pound cocoa powder
- 1 pound butter
- 4 cups of coffee
- 4 cups sugar
- 4 cups flour
- 2 teaspoons baking soda

- 2 teaspoons salt
- 2 teaspoons vanilla extract
- 4 whole eggs
- 24 pieces semi-sweet chocolate
- 1 muffin tray for 12

Preparation

COMBINE cocoa powder, butter, and coffee in a heavy saucepan on medium heat, stirring at all times until all of the butter is incorporated. Do not let it burn.

REMOVE ingredients to a mixing bowl, set with a mixing paddle on low speed. Add the sugar and mix for five minutes, then add flour, baking soda, salt, and vanilla extract and mix for five minutes.

ADD eggs, one at a time, and let mix for three minutes.

BUTTER the muffin cups well, or use a nonstick spray. Fill the muffin cups ¾ of the way with batter mix and place two pieces of the semi-sweet chocolate on top. Use your index finger to push the chocolate to the center of the mix.

BAKE at 350 degrees for 12 minutes, or until done. Let the cake cool completely before taking the muffins out of the tray. To serve, warm for 45 seconds in the microwave and enjoy.

Serves 12

The Fountain Room.

Aix Restaurant

719 E. 17th Ave.
Denver, CO 80203
303-831-1296
www.restaurantaix.com

Dinner
Tuesday - Saturday
5:00 pm – 10:00 pm
Sunday Brunch
10:00 am – 2:00 pm

Aix Restaurant
Cyd Anderson and Rachel Woolcott, Chef Proprietors

Opening in August 2001, Aix Restaurant is a fine addition to the Capitol Hill community. The lively little space has been transformed to give the diner the feeling of its namesake, the small town of Aix-en-Provence in the south of France. This area is know for its special Provencal cooking, a philosophy that espouses the use of fresh ingredients, enhancing the essence of their basic flavors instead of masking them with too many competing tastes.

The interior of Aix hints of the French country charm with its textured sponge-painted walls the color of sun and honey, light wood floors, and a beautiful copper-covered bar. In the summer, the sidewalk patio offers fresh air dining on busy 17th Street.

The Chef Proprietors, Cyd Anderson and Rachel Woolcott have collaborated in a unique way. Each chef takes a turn in the kitchen for a week, while the other manages the front. This alternation seems to help them keep their creative spirit fresh, which shows in the satisfied faces of the diners.

Cyd Anderson received her formal training at the California Culinary Institute, supplementing her training with an apprenticeship at the famous Stars Restaurant in San Francisco. She honed her skills by working with several Napa Valley wineries: Ironhorse, Fetzer, and Chateau Souverain. After coming back to the Denver area, she worked at The Arrowhead Country Club, Cliff Young's, and Barolo Grill. Before opening Aix, Cyd worked at Coors Brewing Company, serving as the private chef to the Coors family.

Rachel Woolcot took a different path. Beginning her culinary experience while attending the University of Colorado at Boulder, she moved to California to work with the chef at the

Ritz-Carlton in Marina del Ray, where the two started a fine dining catering and home chef service. After a stint back in Denver, Rachel decided to further her career by working with some of the finest chefs in Boston, followed by more great training in the San Francisco area.

The diverse training of these two chefs has culminated into a perfect blending in their joint venture. Treat yourself to one of their monthly 4-course wine dinners that are usually held the last Wednesday in every month.

Pear and Endive Salad

A wonderful accompaniment to this dish is candied walnuts.

Ingredients

2 pears
3 endive leaves

1 tablespoon chive, chopped
Creamy Roquefort Dressing
(recipe follows)

Preparation

QUARTER pear and cut in thin slices. Halve lengthwise the endive, lay flat and thinly slice on the bias. Add pear and endive in a mixing bowl and fold in chives.

WHEN ready to serve, pour dressing over ingredients in the bowl and combine.

For Creamy Roquefort Dressing

4 tablespoons Roquefort or Gorgonzola
cheese
1 tablespoon rice wine vinegar or lemon
juice

2 tablespoons walnut oil
chives, chopped
salt and pepper to taste

IN A food processor, add Roquefort cheese, rice wine vinegar, and walnut oil. Pulse until just combined, add chives, and season to taste. This recipe might require a bit more or less walnut oil depending on your own tastes.

Serves 2

AIX 'Award-Winning' Wild Mushroom Soup

A great accompaniment for this dish is fines herbes and white truffle oil sprinkled on top.

Ingredients

1 yellow onion, diced
1 fennel bulb, diced
 olive oil to cook
3 cups portobello mushrooms, sliced
3 cups shiitake mushroom, sliced
3 cups chanterelle mushrooms, sliced

4 tablespoons black truffle peel, chopped
¼ cup sherry vinegar
2 cups chicken stock
2 cups heavy cream
 salt to taste

Preparation

SAUTÉ onion and fennel for five minutes. Add mushrooms over medium heat and cook for about 10 –15 minutes until mushrooms extract all their water. Add truffle peel, sherry, and chicken stock and boil for 3 minutes. Add heavy cream and season and cook over medium heat for about 15 minutes.

Serves 4-6

Aix bar

Country French ambiance.

AIX 'CITY STEAK'

This goes well with mixed greens, potatoes, and fresh vegetables.

Ingredients

4 *10-ounce New York strip steaks*
4 *tablespoons anchovy filet, chopped*
4 *tablespoons black truffle, chopped*
4 *tablespoons parsley, chopped*

4 *tablespoons fines herbes, chopped*
2 *tablespoons garlic, chopped*
    salt and pepper, to taste

Preparation

IN A mixing bowl, combine anchovy, black truffle, parsley, fines herbes, and garlic to make a paste.

SEASON New York strip with salt and pepper on both sides and grill about 3-5 minutes on both sides for medium rare. Spread anchovy-truffle paste over top of one side and let meat rest for 3 minutes before serving.

Serves 4

Sponge-painted walls add warmth.

APPLE TART TATAN

A simple, yet tasty, accompaniment to this dish is a dollop of whipped cream or even crème fraîche (sour cream). For whipped cream, use about ½ cup heavy cream, 2 tablespoons sugar and beat until stiff peaks form.

Ingredients

1¼ cups flour
1 cup plus 1 teaspoon sugar
1 teaspoon salt
¼ pound butter (one stick), small dice

7 Granny Smith apples
⅛ cup ice water
2 tablespoons lemon juice

Preparation

PRE-HEAT oven to 350 degrees.

IN A food processor, combine flour, 1 teaspoon sugar, and salt. While mixing, add butter, one piece at a time, until dough makes 'pebbles'. Knead until dough is smooth. Wrap in a disc shape and chill for 30 minutes.

WHILE dough is chilling, peel the apples and quarter them. Store in water until time to use. In a 14-inch ovenproof cast iron pan, pour in one cup of sugar and heat over medium heat. The sugar will start to melt. Swirl pan as sugar starts to brown so it can cook evenly. When sugar is melted and the color is a deep brown, turn heat off and add the lemon juice to stop the sugar from cooking. Arrange apple quarters starting along the outside in a clockwise fashion. Keep arranging them, working your way to the middle of the pan.

ROLL out dough in a circle shape that's a little larger than the cast iron pan. Place dough over top of pan and apples and tuck in sides. Make a few slits on top to release any steam when cooking and put in the oven for about 20-30 minutes at 350 degrees.

Serves 4-8

Restaurant
Kevin Taylor

KEVIN TAYLOR

1106 14th St.
Denver, CO 80202
303-820-2600
www.restaurantkevintaylor.com

Monday – Saturday
5:30 pm - 10:00 pm
Closed on Sundays

Restaurant Kevin Taylor

Chef and restaurateur Kevin Taylor is an institution in Denver, and has won national acclaim for putting Denver on the culinary map. A native of Colorado, Chef Taylor is known for his creative, unpretentious approach to American cuisine. He has been cooking for more than half of his 40 years, and has owned restaurants in Denver and Boulder for the last 14 years. He began his professional culinary career at age 15, during high school, working weekends and in the summer 12 hours a day. Detail by detail, he learned everything about the kitchen's functions, from butchering to garde manger, from ice carving to making precise sauces. He opened his first restaurant in Denver in 1987 at the age of 25. His career has culminated in the opening of his namesake restaurant in December 1998.

Kevin Taylor's signature dishes are the "tower" dishes, where he combines different textures and colors to create a visually appealing and tasty creation.

His restaurant is located in the Teatro Hotel, a beautifully restored historic landmark next to the Denver Center of Performing Arts. The Teatro Hotel was originally built in 1911 as the Denver Tramway Building. This intimate, luxury venue is highlighted by 17-foot ceilings, with honey-stained pecan wood paneling, gold silk tapestries, and custom-designed furniture and lighting fixtures. Within this opulent design, the dining experience is enhanced with Cristofle silver, Bernardaud china, and Reidel stemware in which his 900 wines are served.

Above the main dining room is an elegant mezzanine bar and dining area, with an open balcony to the dining room below. It's the perfect setting for private parties and small receptions. And for a truly unique and private dining experience, there is an intimate wine cellar with stone tiles, wrought-iron chandeliers, and mahogany wine racks lining the walls.

In the last five years, Chef Kevin Taylor has been cited as a rising star by national magazines and has been a guest chef at the James Beard House in New York City. Each year since opening, Restaurant Kevin Taylor has received the prestigious Mobil Travel Guide's Four-Star rating, the AAA Four-Diamond Award and Wine Spectator's "Best Award of Excellence".

With Kevin Taylor's progressive response to restaurant trends, and his loyalty to a pure, flavor-driven cooking style, his restaurants continue to be recognized as Denver's top dining choices.

Best of Award of Excellence

Teatro's 17-foot ceilings.

Tuna Sashimi "Tower"

with Avocado, Pink Papaya, Pickled Jalapeno, Sweet Soy and Wasabi Tobiko

Ingredients

- 2 jalapenos, seeded
- 2 cups salted water with 1 tablespoon vinegar
- 2 avocados, small dice
- 1 pink papaya, small dice

- 8 ounces sushi grade tuna. small dice
- 2 tablespoons sweet soy sauce
- 2 tablespoons wasabi tobiko caviar
- 5 pickled jalapenos

Preparation

CUT jalapenos into ⅛th inch rings and blanch in salted water with vinegar. Place a ring mold in the center of a medium salad plate. Pack enough of the avocado to go 1/6 of the way up in the ring mold. Next pack the pink papaya on top of the avocado, then the tuna on top of the papaya. This should only fill the ring mold half way. Continue this process again until the top of the ring mold is packed with tuna. Spoon some wasabi tobiko on top of the tuna. Remove the ring, and drag the sweet soy around the tower of tuna with a small spoon. Garnish the plate with the pickled jalapenos, and serve.

Serves 4

Wine Suggestion: Riesling Spatlese, Joseph Leitz, Germany 2002 - This is a high acidity wine with virtually no oak, which complements the leanness of the tuna and the spice of the jalapeno

Tuna Sashimi "Tower"

Restaurant Kevin Taylor, Denver

Potato Crusted Halibut
with Crisp Potato Cake, Creamed Spinach

Ingredients

4 4-ounce portions halibut
6 potatoes
4 tablespoons butter
1 bottle red wine, reduced by two-thirds

4 cups baby spinach
1 cup heavy cream
½ pound unsalted butter
   fresh herbs for garnish

Preparation

CUT the potatoes into quarter size cylinders. Slice them thin, using a mandolin, and toss in 2 tablespoons butter. Spiral the potatoes three layers high in a small blini or high-sided ovenproof pan. Place on a medium heat, brown the bottom, and finish in 400 degree oven for 4-6 minutes.

CLARIFY two tablespoons butter. Place some of the potato discs over the halibut filet to resemble scales. Sear in a hot sauté pan with clarified butter. Once the potatoes begin to brown, scale the backside of the filet, and brown the other side. Place in a 400 degree oven, and cook for 3-5 minutes. In a large sauté pan over high heat, sauté the spinach and finish with cream. Place the red wine reduction in a small saucepan, bring to a boil, and finish with unsalted butter.

PLACE the remaining potato cake in the center of a large bowl. Top the cake with creamed spinach, and lay the crusted halibut over the spinach. Spoon the red wine sauce around the potato cake, and garnish with fresh herbs.

Serves 4

Wine Suggestion: Pinot Noir, Hartford, Sonoma Coast 2000 - This wine has great balance between its fruit and earthiness, which counterpoints the richness of the red wine sauce and the earthy flavor of the potatoes.

ATLANTIC SALMON "FILET MIGNON"

Ingredients

4 5-ounce portions of salmon
2 large Yukon gold potatoes
12 green asparagus, peeled
8 white asparagus, peeled
4 chives, blanched

2 tablespoons clarified butter
salt and pepper to taste
oil to season
Herb Mousseline (recipe follows)

Preparation

CUT salmon thin, roll to form filet, and tie. Boil potatoes until fork tender, and cut in half.

PREHEAT oven to 400 degrees. To make asparagus bundles, place 3 green asparagus and 2 white asparagus together and tie with 1 chive. Keep refrigerated.

SEASON a sheet tray with clarified butter, salt and pepper, and place the halved potatoes, cut side down, on the tray. Place in oven for 4-6 minutes, or until the potatoes are browned. Remove from oven, and keep in a warm area until needed.

SEASON both sides of the salmon filets with oil, salt and pepper. Grill both sides and finish in oven until medium rare (3-5 minutes, depending on thickness). Place the asparagus bundles in the steamer, or a pot of boiling water for 2 minutes, or until soft. Season with salt and pepper and keep warm. Make the mousseline.

ASSEMBLE by placing the potato, cut side up, in the center of a large entrée plate. Place the salmon on top of the potato, making sure to remove the butcher's twine, and garnish with one bundle of asparagus over the fish. Blend the mousseline, check for seasoning, and spoon around the potato.

Atlantic Salmon "Filet Mignon"

Restaurant Kevin Taylor, Denver

Atlantic Salmon "Filet Mignon"
CONTINUED

For Herb Mousseline

¼ cup herbs (chervil, tarragon, parsley, and chives)
1 cup beurre blanc

½ cup crème fraîche, whipped stiff
1 egg
salt and pepper to taste

BLANCH herbs in salted water and puree. Place the beurre blanc in a small frothing pitcher. Add the puree of herbs, crème fraîche, and egg. Season with salt and pepper, and puree with hand blender. Mousseline should be thick and bubbly.

Serves 4

Wine Suggestion: Sauvignon Blanc, Nobilo, ICON Marlborough New Zealand
This fuller bodied Sauvignon Blanc complements the creaminess of the beurre blanc and has just enough acidity to cut the richness of the salmon.

Interior shot of Kevin Taylor's dining room.

Entrance.

RACK OF COLORADO LAMB
with Couscous, Medjool Dates and Cardamom Jus

Ingredients

4 2½ ounce portions rack of lamb	½ yellow onion, minced
5 ounces leg of lamb	1 tablespoon butter
flour to dredge	2 cups couscous
olive oil for cooking	1 teaspoon coriander
1 carrot, rough chop	1 teaspoon cumin
1 celery, rough chop	1 teaspoon cardamom
1 onion, rough chop	½ teaspoon turmeric
2 tablespoons tomato paste	½ teaspoon cayenne pepper
1 sprig rosemary	boiling water to cover
½ bottle red wine	12 medjool dates, pitted
water to cover	3 cardamom pods, toasted and ground

Preparation

DREDGE the leg of lamb in flour, and brown in olive oil over high heat. Place in small baking pan, and set aside. In a small stockpot, sauté the carrot, celery, and onion over high heat until browned. Add the tomato paste, and rosemary, and mix well. When the bottom of the pan begins to brown, add a little red wine at a time until a reduction has been made, and all of the wine has been incorporated. Place this reduction over the leg of lamb, and top with water. Cover with aluminum foil, and braise in 300 degree oven for 3½ hours. Remove from liquid, shred fine with fingers, and pour a small amount of liquid back over the meat to keep moist. Place in warm area until needed. Reserve the remaining lamb sauce for serving.

TO MAKE the couscous, sauté the minced onion in a small amount of butter until translucent. Place in a small mixing bowl with couscous, coriander, cumin, cardamom, turmeric and cayenne. Top with just enough boiling water to cover the couscous. Place plastic wrap over the bowl and let sit for 10 minutes. Remove the plastic wrap, and fluff the couscous with fork. Keep warm and set aside.

SEASON and sear the rack of lamb on all sides, and finish in 400 degree oven until medium rare. (5-7 minutes). Place a 3 inch ring mold in the center of a large entrée plate, and pack the couscous into the ring. Remove the mold, and spoon the shredded leg of lamb over the couscous. Slice the rack of lamb into two pieces and lay over the shredded leg. Warm the dates in the oven, and place three around the couscous. Add the toasted, ground cardamom to the lamb sauce, and spoon around the lamb.

Serves 2-4

Wine Suggestion: LeVolte, Ornellaia, Tuscany 2000 - A really luscious, heady, earthy wine – a perfect match for this dish.

BROKEN ARROW RANCH VENISON
with Roasted Pear, Butternut Squash, Criminis and a Black Pepper Jus

Ingredients

4 5-ounce portions Broken Arrow Ranch
   venison, seasoned with rough cracked
   pepper
2 pears, peeled and cored
1 cup simple syrup (1 part water, 2
   parts sugar)
1 sprig rosemary
1 butternut squash
1 tablespoon brown sugar
2 tablespoons butter

½ white onion, julienned
1 tablespoon oil
1 banana
   salt and pepper to taste
1 tablespoon sugar
1 tablespoon butter
10 crimini mushrooms, quartered and
   sautéed in garlic oil
   fresh herbs for garnish

Preparation

SIMMER the pears in simple syrup and rosemary until fork tender. Split, clean, and roast squash in low oven with brown sugar and butter until soft. Sauté the onion in oil until caramelized. Scoop the cooked squash from the skin and place in a food processor with the banana, and caramelized onion. Puree smooth, and season with salt and pepper. Keep warm until serving.

SEAR the venison in a hot sauté pan on both sides, and finish in oven (should be cooked medium rare). Cut the pears into two halves, and caramelize in a hot sauté pan with sugar and butter. Place a large quenelle of butternut squash puree in the center of a large entrée plate, and spoon a small amount of the sauteed crimini mushrooms around. Slice the venison into 5-6 pieces, and fan to one side. Keeping the half pear in one piece, slice four times, and fan on the other side of the squash. Garnish with fresh herbs.

Serves 4

Wine Suggestion: Stag's Leap Petit Syrah - This wine has big fruit and spice, making it gutsy enough to stand up to the predominant black pepper of the dish.

Rocky Mountain Diner

800 18th St.
Denver, CO 80202
303-293-8383
www.rockymountaindiner.com

Sunday – Thursday
11:00 am – 10:00 pm
Friday – Saturday
11:00 am – 11:00 pm

Rocky Mountain Diner

Locals call it "The Diner," and western comfort food has been a specialty since 1990. In the heart of downtown Denver, the Diner is a bright, busy place with a strong western theme throughout. A sign on the front door says "Get in Here!" - and when do, you know immediately that this is the place for homemade, tummy-warming food.

Denver architect William Lang designed the Ghost building, which houses the Diner, in the late 1800's for A.H. Ghost. In 1974, the building was dismantled and each stone in the stone façade was individually numbered before being stored for a decade. When the building was reassembled, Brown-Shrepferman's construction team used the original details and modern materials to recreated the historic building.

A twist on the traditional favorite, the buffalo meatloaf (recipe included in this chapter), joins Yankee pot roast, chicken fried steak, and an open-faced hot turkey sandwich on Fiesta Ware. Everything under the roof is prepared fresh daily with quality ingredients under the watchful eye of Executive Chef Michael Naumann.

The restaurant's logo, a sheriff's badge, is prominent on the front of the menu, which includes an instruction to "check your guns at the bar". An antler chandelier at the entrance illuminates the brightly colored western art on the walls. The wood tables have seared brands, the lighted onyx topped bar has two authentic horse saddles, which are used as bar stools, and there is a vintage Remington casting displayed at the host stand to greet visitors. The row of windows along 18th offers a view of the old main post office, a Greek style white marble building, and the bighorn sheep sculpted by Gladys Caldwell Fisher.

The Diner raises your expectations for old-fashioned western food and hospitality and doesn't disappoint.

Comfort food is a Diner specialty.

DUCK ENCHILADAS

Ingredients

2 corn tortillas	Tomatillo Chipotle Sauce
3 ounces Havarti cheese	(recipe follows)
3 ounces roasted duck breast meat, julienned	Roasted Corn Salsa (recipe follows)
½ cup black beans	⅛ cup sour cream
	6-8 pickled jalapeño rings
	1 tablespoon scallions

Preparation

FLASH fry tortillas to soften. Place equal portions of the cheese and the duck meat on each tortilla. Broil to heat and melt cheese. Roll enchiladas and place on serving dish. Ladle ½ cup of the tomatillo-chipotle sauce around tortillas with black beans to one side. Garnish with ⅓ cup roasted corn salsa, sour cream, jalapeno rings, and scallions.

For the Tomatillo Chipotle Sauce

1 pound tomatillos, charred	1-2 chipotle peppers
2 tablespoons margarine, melted	1 lime, juiced
¼ pound onions, chopped	½ bunch parsley
1 tablespoon garlic, minced	1 teaspoon salt
	2 cups St. Louis style BBQ sauce

COMBINE all ingredients in a blender and mix until pureed. Extra sauce can be stored in refrigerator.

Roasted Corn Salsa

1 cup corn kernels	1 jalapeno, diced
2 teaspoons sugar	1 tablespoon lemon juice
pinch of salt	1 teaspoon garlic, minced
1 cup tomatoes, diced	2 tablespoons cilantro, chopped
¼ cup onion, diced	1 teaspoon salt

ROAST corn, sugar, and salt in oven until slightly caramelized. Combine all ingredients and set aside. There will be extra left over.

Serves 1

BUFFALO MEATLOAF

Ingredients

3   pounds ground buffalo
1   stick butter
¾   pounds onions, diced
¼   pound celery, diced
2   eggs
1   cup bread crumbs

½   cup milk
½   tablespoon thyme
½   tablespoon salt
½   tablespoon black pepper
½   tablespoon garlic powder

Preparation

SAUTÉ butter, onions, and celery. Combine eggs, bread crumbs, and milk and add to buffalo, thyme, salt, pepper, and garlic powder.

USING a mixer, or by hand if you prefer, combine all ingredients until blended. Place in loaf pans and bake at 325 degrees until meat reaches an internal temperature of 160 degrees. Goes well with mashed potatoes, brown onion gravy, and a vegetable medley.

Serves 8–10

Saddle seating at the bar.

BANANA CREAM PIE

Ingredients

1 9-inch graham cracker pie crust
3 ounces semi-sweet chocolate
1 tablespoon whipping cream
2 fresh bananas, sliced
2 tablespoons pineapple juice
2 pounds vanilla custard, chilled

2 cups whipping cream
2 tablespoons powdered sugar
1 teaspoon vanilla
white chocolate shavings for garnish
cocoa powder for garnish

Preparation

COMBINE and microwave chocolate and whipping cream. Pour into crust and chill.

TOSS the bananas with the pineapple juice, then put the bananas into the chilled crust.

PLACE the custard on top of bananas, and, using pasty knife, form custard into a slight mound.

WHIP cream, powered sugar and vanilla to stiff peaks. Place whipped cream on top of custard and form into same mound shape. Garnish top of pie with white chocolate shavings and cocoa powder.

Serves 6-8

Denver Wheel Club. Men and bicycles crowd the front of a house in Denver. (between 1890 and 1910)

Samba Room

CUBAN BAR

SAMBA·ROOM

1460 Larimer Street
Denver, CO 80202
720-956-1701
www.e-brands.net

Monday -Wednesday
11:00 am –11:00 pm
Thursday - Saturday
11:00 am - Midnight
Sunday
11:00 am –10:00 pm

The Samba Room

In March of 2002 The Samba Room restaurant opened in Larimer Square in Denver. Larimer Square is the oldest and most historic block in the city, rich in history and legend. The discovery of gold in 1858 in the Pike's Peak area brought hopefuls to Colorado, among them General William H. Larimer Jr. from Kansas.

Larimer Square was home to Denver's first bank, bookstore, photographer and dry goods store, as well as the first post office. It was the hub of activity and still is today, as it's located just three blocks from the Colorado Convention Center, two blocks from the Denver Performing Arts Complex, close to the 16th Street Mall shuttle, across the street from the Pepsi Center and near Coors Field.

The Samba Room offers creative Latin fusion cuisine in a warm, energetic atmosphere. The vibrant murals, café tables, and booths are complemented by the serpentine bar and gauzy curtains adorning the main dining room. Executive Chef and General Manager Tim Maness brings together Caribbean, Cuban, and South American food in a multi-cultural collection of over 30 dishes.

Tim trained at the California Culinary Institute in San Francisco, and has over 10 years of experience preparing food that combines his passion for fresh ingredients with a flair for the unusual.

From the crispy plantain chips to the jerk chicken, the menu reflects the Latin influence on fresh seafood, grilled meats, and salads. The music contributes to the mood with Afro-Cuban jazz and Brazilian rhythms.

The wine list includes a variety of vintages, primarily from South America and California. Mambo-inspired cocktails are part of the ambiance, and the signature Mojito, which is included in the following recipes, is considered by many to be the best Cuban cocktail in existence.

The menu offers items like Argentinean-style skirt steak with classic sauces and papas fritas, sautéed shrimp and chicken in coconut broth with toasted cashews and whole red snapper crispy fried with green rice and garlic ginger broth. A tapas menu is also available seven days a week.

The Samba Room is an experience for all five senses.

Samba Room's dining area.

Samba Room, Denver

MOJITO

In Spanish, mojito is "to wet." This Cuban classic is also a Samba Room specialty!

Ingredients

¼ cup sugarcane juice
1 teaspoon sugar
1½ ounces light rum (best quality)
1 teaspoon fresh squeezed lime juice
5 fresh mint leaves

crushed ice
splash of 7-Up to taste
1 stick of sugarcane
1 lime wheel

Preparation

PLACE sugarcane juice and sugar, rum, lime, and mint in a shaker. Add crushed ice and shake vigorously to release the mint oils. Fill a rocks glass with ice and pour the cocktail over ice. Top with 7-Up and stir with the sugarcane stick. Garnish with lime wheel.

Serves 1

HONDURAN CEVICHE

The Central American country of Honduras grows and exports coconuts and is famous for its ceviches, and other seafood snacks. The presentation in coconut shells offers a dramatic and unusual twist to serve to your friends. The Samba Room often has ceviche on the menu, depending on availability. (Use only Grade A sushi-quality tuna for this recipe).

Ingredients

1 coconut
1 jalapeno chile, chopped with seeds
2 tablespoons gingerroot, chopped
3 tablespoons Oriental fish sauce
1 tablespoon sugar
½ cup freshly squeezed lime juice
1 can (14 ounces) unsweetened coconut milk
1½ pounds sushi quality fresh tuna, cut into ¼ inch dice
½ red onion, thinly sliced into half-moons

2 tablespoons scallions, sliced
1 tablespoon chives, finely chopped
3 tablespoons fresh cilantro leaves, finely chopped
¼ cup shaved coconut
½ cup red bell pepper, seeded and diced
1 bunch watercress, leaves only
2 cups shaved coconut
Mariquitas (fried plantain chips-recipe follows)

HONDURAN CEVICHE
CONTINUED

Preparation

THE coconut is for the serving dish. Using the back of a heavy knife, whack the coconut along its middle, while rotating it in your hand, until it splits open. Pat the insides of the coconut dry, shave coconut meat, and set aside in refrigerator.

PLACE the jalapeno, gingerroot, fish sauce, sugar, lime juice, and coconut milk in a blender and puree until smooth. When you are ready to serve, toss with the tuna. Then, at the last minute, sprinkle with the onion, scallions, chives, cilantro, and shaved coconut. Place mixture in the coconut halves and garnish with equal portions of plantain chips, bell pepper, watercress leaves, and shaved coconut.

For Mariquitas

3 cups canola oil	1 tablespoon cumin
6 tablespoons sugar	6 green plantains
1 tablespoon fresh ground black pepper	

PEEL plantains and slice lengthwise, using a mandolin. Heat the oil to 350 degrees in a deep fryer or heavy bottomed saucepan. Immediately add the plantain chips one at a time. Be careful not to overload the pan, as the oil will not stay hot enough, you may have to cook in batches. Deep fry until golden brown, about 3-4 minutes.

REMOVE the chips with a wire-mesh strainer and drain on paper towels. Mix together sugar, pepper, and cumin. Sprinkle mixture over chips and let cool.

Serves 8

Roasted Pear, Red Onion, and Walnut Salsa

A great alternative to salad dressing, also great served over grilled fish or lamb.

Ingredients

- 1 large red onion, quartered
- 3 Bartlett pears, peeled, cored, and seeded
- 1 tablespoon organic honey
- ½ teaspoon ground cinnamon
- ½ teaspoon allspice

- juice of 3 limes
- 1 tablespoon chopped chives
- ½ cup chopped walnuts, toasted
- ¼ cup walnut oil
- 1 tablespoon chopped fresh cilantro

Preparation

PRE-HEAT oven to 400 degrees.

PLACE onions and pears on baking sheet in oven until edges are brown and caramelized, about 25 minutes. Remove from oven and let cool for one hour, uncovered. Dice onions and pears and transfer to a mixing bowl. Add remaining ingredients and combine. Refrigerate for at least one hour before serving.

Serves 4-8

GRILLED AHI TUNA WITH MANGO-GINGER MOJO

Ingredients

6 5-6 ounce fresh ahi tuna steaks, 1½
   inches thick
1 cup mango juice
½ teaspoon fresh ginger, minced,
2 fresh mangoes, peeled, diced
3 green onions, sliced thin
1 red bell pepper, diced
2 tablespoons dried mango, diced

1 teaspoon crystallized ginger, minced
¼ cup fresh squeezed lime juice
2 tablespoons fresh cilantro, minced
1 jalapeno or Serrano chile, diced
¼ cup canola oil
   kosher salt
   ground black pepper

Preparation

FOR the mojo, combine mango juice and ginger in a saucepan and bring to a boil. Continue boiling and reduce by half, approximately 5-8 minutes. Remove and let cool completely. Add the diced mango, green onions, bell peppers, dried mango, crystallized ginger, lime juice, cilantro, chile, and oil. Season the mojo ingredients with salt and pepper to taste. Set aside.

PREPARE the grill, medium fire, and oil the grates well. Oil and season the tuna steaks with salt and pepper. Arrange on hot grill grates. Grill two minutes per side, keeping steak rare.

TRANSFER tuna to serving plate, spoon mojo over warm fish. Serve immediately.

Serves 6

Wine suggestion: Hogue Fruit Forward Chardonnay, Columbia Valley Chardonnay

APPLE SORBET

This is a light, refreshing dessert. The recipe works best with Granny Smith apples, because they produce the freshest tasting sorbet. The dessert menu at the Samba Room always carries sorbet, with the flavors rotating with the seasons.

Ingredients

½ cup sugar
1 cup water
½ cup light corn syrup
2 drops green food coloring (optional)
  juice of 2 lemons

15 Granny Smith apples, peeled, cored,
  and cut into 1 inch cubes
2 Granny Smith apples, unpeeled and
  thinly sliced for garnish

Preparation

COMBINE the sugar and water together in a heavy bottomed saucepan and bring to a strong boil, without stirring. Remove from the heat and let cool. Transfer to a mixing bowl, add the corn syrup, food coloring, and lemon juice, mix well.

JUICE the apple cubes in a juice extractor and stir the juice into the sugar mixture. Pour into the container of an ice cream machine and freeze according to the manufacturer's directions. Garnish with the apple slices.

Serves 2–4

Barbecue at the Denver Union Stockyard. (between 1897 and 1910)

Strings

strings

1700 Humboldt St.
Denver, CO 80218
303-831-7310
www.stringsrestaurant.com

Monday – Thursday
11:00 am – 10:00 pm
Friday and Saturday
11:00 am – 10:30 pm
Sunday
5:00 pm – 10:00 pm

Strings
Noel Cunningham, Owner
Amy Vitale, Chef

It's no surprise Noel Cunningham went into the restaurant business. His father was a chef at the Grasham Hotel – Dubin's equivalent to London's Savoy Hotel – his uncle was executive chef for all Aerlinges operations at Dublin Airport. His mother, aunts, and uncles also worked in the food business as chefs, waitresses, and bartenders.

Noel went to work for his uncle at a young age, due to health problems that sidelined his schooling, and he learned quickly. After three and a half years, he moved to London, where he was hired as an apprentice at the famous Savoy Hotel. He went to culinary school and became a sous chef at the Savoy at age 24 – the youngest person to reach that rank, an especially notable achievement since he is not French.

After moving to California, Noel become the sous chef at Touch, a supper club in Beverly Hills, then he went to Denver and opened Strings in 1986.

His mother instilled in Noel a desire to help others, and he is very involved in the Share Our Strength organization, helping the hungry and homeless. Quarters For Kids was started by Noel and Tammy in 1990, and is built on the concept of `kids helping kids'. Over 114,000 quarters have been raised since the program began. Noel also is involved with Project Mercy, Meals on Wheels, Project Safeguard, Hospice of Cincinnati and other worthy causes.

Strings is a Denver favorite. Noel's gracious and caring attitude infuses the restaurant. The staff is welcoming and makes you glad you came. The food is seasonal, with such delightful offerings as cashew-crusted sea bass, penne bagutta, and roasted red pepper tomato bisque. The wine list offers some of the best wines from around the world.

Seating is conducive for conversation, and private rooms for groups of 10-100 people are available.

The atrium.

Zuppa de Pesce

Ingredients

4 ounces olive oil	6 tomatoes, peeled and diced
½ shallot	1 cup white wine
1 teaspoon minced garlic	1 cup clam juice
12 13/15 shrimp	1 tablespoon brunoise
8 ounces mixed fish	(carrot, celery, leek)
12 medium scallops	1 teaspoon red pepper flakes
16 clams	salt and white pepper to taste
16 mussels	2 ounces angel hair pasta

Preparation

COMBINE olive oil, shallot, and garlic in large sauté pan. Heat and add shrimp, fish, and scallops. After three minutes add clams, mussels, and tomatoes. Sauté, then add white wine, clam juice, and brunoise vegetables. Reduce. Add red pepper flakes, salt, and pepper to taste. Place pasta in boiling water and cook until al dente (about four minutes).
Make sure all clams and mussels have opened, and serve over cooked pasta.

Serves 4

Wine suggestion: R.H. Phillips "E.X.P." Viognier 2001 California

Strings exterior at night.

SEARED HALIBUT
with Celery Root Puree

Ingredients

4 6-7 ounce halibut filets
½ cup flour
    salt and pepper to taste
1 tablespoon butter
1 teaspoon lemon juice

Celery Root Puree (recipe follows)
Spicy Bloody Mary sauce
(recipe follows)
4 Kumomoto oysters

Preparation

PLACE halibut filets in flour and season with salt and pepper. Shake off excess flour and place in hot skillet with butter and lemon. Flip halibut after about 30 seconds and place in oven for about four minutes.

TO SERVE, set halibut on top of celery root puree and drizzle spicy Bloody Mary sauce around plate. Place one Kumomoto oyster on top of halibut.

For Spicy Bloody Mary Sauce

1 tablespoon celery salt
1 tablespoon Worcestershire sauce
3 tablespoons horseradish
½ cup vodka
½ cup tomatoes, coarsely chopped
½ cup tomato juice

¼ cup tomato sauce
    salt
    fresh cracked black pepper
    Tabasco
    horseradish

COMBINE and reduce first four ingredients. Add the tomatoes, tomato juice and tomato sauce and simmer. Season with salt, pepper, Tabasco, and horseradish to taste.

For Celery Root Puree

2 each celery root
    lemon juice to cover
¼ pound butter

¼ cup cream
    salt and pepper to taste

PEEL, wash, and dice celery root. Boil celery root with lemon juice until tender. Strain, then put into blender with butter, cream, and salt and pepper to taste. Blend until smooth.

Serves 4

Wine suggestion: 2001 Foris "Rogue Valley" Gewurztraminer, Oregon

TENDERLOIN
with Blue Cheese Gratin Tomato Jam and Burgundy Demi-Glace

Ingredients

8 10-ounce tenderloin cuts
¼ cup olive oil
   salt and pepper

Burgundy Demi (recipe follows)
Tomato Jam (recipe follows)
Bingham Hill Gratin (recipe follows)

Preparation

PREPARE burgundy demi, tomato jam, and gratin.

OIL and season each tenderloin. Place on hot grill. Cook on each side for about five minutes for medium rare, or sauté. To sauté, get skillet hot with oil. Place tenderloins in skillet, cook for about three minutes on stovetop. Turn tenderloins over and place in 350-degree oven for about 8-10 minutes for medium rare.

TO SERVE, place ⅛ of the gratin on each plate, with ⅛TH of tomato jam. Place one tenderloin on plate and drizzle burgundy demi over tenderloin.

For the Burgundy Demi

2 shallots
10 whole black peppercorns
3 springs fresh thyme
1 cup + 1 dash red wine

2 cups veal stock or beef base
¼ cup butter
   salt and pepper to taste

COMBINE and reduce the first four ingredients by three-quarters. Add veal stock or beef base and reduce again by half. Strain. Add butter and an additional dash of red wine. Whisk, add salt and pepper to taste.

For the Tomato Jam

10 plum tomatoes, coarsely chopped
1 cinnamon stick
1 bay leaf

2 tablespoons red wine vinegar
¼ cup sugar

COMBINE ingredients and simmer. Makes four cups.

TENDERLOIN
with Blue Cheese Gratin Tomato Jam and Burgundy Demi-Glace
CONTINUED

For the Bingham Hill Gratin

- 4 large Idaho potatoes
- 2 eggs
- ¼ cup heavy cream
- ½ cup blue cheese

- ½ cup Parmesan cheese
- salt and pepper
- butter

COMBINE eggs, heavy cream, blue cheese and a quarter cup of Parmesan cheese in a bowl. Whisk together, salt and pepper to taste, and set aside. Slice potatoes very thin and add to mixture.

BUTTER one 6 x 9 or similar-sized baking pan.

PLACE mixture evenly in pan and place remaining ¼ cup of Parmesan cheese on top. Cover with foil. Place in water bath.

COOK for one hour in a 450-degree oven. Remove cover and cook until brown.

Serves 8

Wine suggestion: Ferrari Carano Merlot 2000 Sonoma, Niebaum-Coppola "Cask" Cabernet Sauvignon 1998 Napa

Tenderloin

Fourth Story

Above The Tattered Cover
2955 East First Avenue
Denver, CO 80206
303-322-1824
www.fourthstory.com

Lunch
Monday – Saturday
11:00 am – 4:00 pm
Dinner
Monday – Saturday
5:00 pm – 10:00 pm
Sunday Brunch
10:30 am – 2:30 pm

Fourth Story Restaurant & Bar
Christopher Reap, Chef

In 1995, the Tattered Cover Book Store, a three-story booklover's paradise in Denver for 30 years, expanded to include fine food on the top floor. The exquisite setting of warm cherry wood, loaded bookshelves, overstuffed chairs, and a beautiful view of the Rocky Mountains is appropriately named the Fourth Story Restaurant.

The freshest fish, seafood, poultry, aged steaks, and delectable pastas define Chef Christopher Reap's refined, rustic cuisine. Chef Reap was the Executive Chef for Nicois in Denver, and the Aspen Mountain Club in Aspen, as well as visiting chef for the "21" Club in New York, Harry's Bar in London, England, Hotel Splendido in Portofino, Italy, and the Villa San Micele in Florence, Italy. Chef Reap's creations include entrees such as Wild Mushroom Ragout, Roasted Black Sea Bass, and Pan Roasted Veal Tenderloin. The food is complimented by a wine list distinguished by the Wine Spectator's Award of Excellence.

The Fourth Story's smoke-free bar is a popular gathering place for Denver locals. The classic cocktails, amazing selection of wines by the glass, and friendly, knowledgeable bartenders make it one of the best "bars for dining" in town. A private dining room is available for special events. The room has eight-foot arched windows with a view of Pike's Peak and the Front Range.

The restaurant is open for lunch, dinner, and Sunday brunch, complete with live music. Jazz and classic cocktails kick off the workweek every Monday night. The restaurant hosts an ongoing series of Winemaker Dinners, Wine & Cheese pairings, Tea Tastings and exhibits by local artists on a regular basis.

Some of the recent awards the Fourth Story Restaurant has received are "Top New American Bistro" from Rocky Mountain News Dining Guide, March 2003; "Top Weekend Brunch" from Rocky Mountain News, Top of the Rocky, October 2003; and one of the "Top Six Places for Breakfast or Lunch" from 5280 magazine, Dining in Denver issue, December 2003/January 2004.

Y Award of Excellence

BRINED PORK LOIN
with Roasted Apples, Mustard Greens, Smoked Bacon, and White Cheddar Grits

Ingredients

4 7-8 ounce loins, boneless
4 strips smoked bacon
¼ pound mustard greens
5 cups water
1 cup brown sugar
1 cup kosher salt
2 bay leaves
10 black peppercorns

6 juniper berries
   salt and pepper to taste
   olive oil for cooking
2 Rome apples, cored and cut into 6
   wedges
   White Cheddar Grits (recipe follows)
   Sauce (recipe follows)

Preparation

CUT the smoked bacon crosswise, ⅛ inch thick, and sauté until crisp and brown. Strain off bacon drippings and reserve, let bacon drain on paper towels. Clean mustard greens, remove any thick stems, wash, and pat dry, reserve.

TO PREPARE the brine, combine water, brown sugar, kosher salt, bay leaves, black peppercorns, and juniper berries in a large saucepan, bring to a boil, simmer for 20 minutes, strain, and cool. Submerge the portioned pork in the cool brine for 1 to 2 hours. While pork is brining, prepare the grits.

PREHEAT oven to 375 degrees. Season pork with cracked black pepper, sear in hot sauté pan with olive oil on both sides until golden brown, strain off oil and reserve. Add apples to pan and place in oven. Cook for 6 to 8 minutes, turn pork and apples, and continue to cook for 6 to 8 minutes, or internal temperature reaches 140 degrees (for medium). Remove pork and apples from pan and keep warm. Add reserved oil to sauce, return pan to heat, add reserved bacon drippings, and heat. Add mustard greens and sauté until tender, season as necessary. Spoon grits into large bowl, slice pork in half, top with mustard greens, apple wedges and drizzle with sauce.

For the White Cheddar Grits

2½ cups water
1 cup grits
1 tablespoon butter

1¼ cups white cheddar cheese
   salt and pepper to taste

BRINED PORK LOIN
with Roasted Apples, Mustard Greens, Smoked Bacon, and White Cheddar Grits
CONTINUED

BRING water to a boil in a large saucepan, whisk in the grits slowly, simmer until tender and smooth. Add butter, cheese and salt and black pepper to taste. If necessary, add milk or water to adjust consistency.

For the Sauce

3 tablespoons butter	2 sprigs fresh thyme
2 large shallots, sliced	3 cups chicken stock or low sodium
3 Granny Smith apples, diced	canned chicken broth
1 cup Calvados or apple brandy	1 tablespoon whole grain mustard
2 cups white wine	

HEAT 1 tablespoon butter over medium heat in a medium size saucepan, add shallots, and cook until tender. Add apples and cook for five minutes, stirring frequently. Add Calvados, white wine and fresh thyme. Lower heat to a simmer and reduce by ¾, add chicken stock reduce by ½, strain into a small saucepan, add mustard and stir in remaining butter over low heat, adjust seasoning with salt and black pepper to taste. Hold sauce in a warm place for service.

Serves 4

Wine Pairing: Toad Hollow '00 Merlot Reserve

The Fourth Story's bar.

DUCK CONFIT POT PIE
with Wild Berry Sauce

Ingredients

1 pound picked duck confit
(from gourmet store, such as Dean &
Deluca)
¾ cup butter
½ cup diced carrots
½ cup diced parsnips
½ cup diced potatoes
¼ cup red pearl onions
¼ cup white pearl onions

1 tablespoon chopped fresh thyme
½ cup Calvados
3 cups chicken stock or low sodium
broth
½ cup all purpose flour
½ pound pie dough or puff pastry sheets
1 egg, whipped
Wild Berry Sauce (recipe follows)

Preparation

MELT butter in a large sauté pan, pour off a ½ cup of the butter and reserve. Heat the remaining butter to medium heat. Add the carrots and parsnips and sauté for five minutes, add remaining vegetables and continue cooking until browned and tender. Add fresh thyme and cook for one minute.

REMOVE vegetable mixture from pan, cool mixture slightly and fold in duck. De-glaze sauté pan with Calvados. Add vegetable-duck mixture back to pan, add chicken stock or broth, and bring to a simmer.

IN A separate pan add reserved butter, warm and then mix in flour to create a roux, stirring until smooth. Continue to cook for ten minutes, stirring frequently. Add roux to simmering duck mixture in tablespoon increments until desired consistency is achieved. Continue to simmer mixture for ten minutes, stirring frequently. Season with salt and pepper, remove from heat and let cool, refrigerated.

LINE buttered individual ramekins or single pie pan with dough, add mixture, and cover with dough. Poke holes in dough with a sharp knife, brush top with whipped egg and bake at 350 degrees for 35 to 40 minutes, until golden brown. Serve with warm wild berry sauce.

DUCK CONFIT POT PIE
with Wild Berry Sauce
CONTINUED

For the Wild Berry Sauce

½ cup dried huckleberries or blueberries
1 tablespoon butter
1 large shallot, chopped
½ tablespoon rice wine vinegar

1 cup chicken stock, warm
¼ cup sugar
1 teaspoon molasses
   salt and pepper to taste

HEAT butter in saucepan, add shallot, and cook until translucent. Add rice wine vinegar, berries, and chicken stock or broth. Simmer for 10 minutes, add sugar and molasses, and continue to simmer for an additional 5 minutes. Puree mixture in a blender until smooth. Add additional stock or broth if needed to reach desired consistency. Season with salt and pepper. Reserve for service.

Serves 4

Wine Pairing: Ravenswood '01 "Icon" Syrah

GRILLED QUAIL
with Corn and Morel Spoon Bread, Maple and Currants

Ingredients

4 each semi-boneless quail
1 large shallot, minced
1 tablespoon sherry vinegar
1 teaspoon chopped fresh rosemary
1 tablespoon cracked black pepper
1 tablespoon maple syrup

2 tablespoons olive oil
   Spoon Bread (recipe follows)
   Maple Currant Sauce (recipe follows)
   chopped chives or fresh herb for
   garnish

Preparation

MIX the shallot, sherry vinegar, rosemary, and black pepper together. Let rest for 1 hour at room temperature, then add maple syrup and olive oil. Whisk until well incorporated, add quail, and let marinate for 1 to 2 hours, tossing every half hour. Remove from marinade and reserve under refrigeration for service.

SEASON the quail with salt, and grill or pan sear it, breast side down, for 5 to 7 minutes. Use medium flame, if grilled, and medium high heat if pan seared. Turn quail and cook an additional 2 to 3 minutes or until desired temperature is reached. It's best if served medium rare to medium. Remove from heat and let rest in a warm place.

TO SERVE, remove spoon bread from oven, spoon out desired portion, top with quail, and drizzle with sauce. Garnish with chopped chives or desired fresh herb. This dish can also be served as a main course by adding additional quail.

For the Spoon Bread

1 cup mushrooms (assorted chanterelles, criminis, oyster)	5 tablespoons butter
¼ cup olive oil	1 teaspoon salt
salt and cracked black pepper to taste	1 cup milk
2 cups water	2 large eggs, whipped
1 cup cornmeal	¼ cup chopped chives
	½ cup grated Parmesan cheese

PREHEAT oven to 350 degrees. Toss mushrooms in the olive oil, salt and cracked black pepper, roast in oven until tender. Remove from oven and cool on a cookie sheet. For the spoon bread, put water in a medium-sized saucepan, bring to a boil. Add the cornmeal in to the pot slowly, mix well with a whisk until smooth, and add butter and salt. Remove from heat, add milk, and then eggs, mixing rapidly as to not cook the eggs. Finish with chives, roasted mushrooms, and Parmesan. Place mixture in appropriately sized buttered casserole dish, place dish in a water bath, and cook at 350 degrees for 35 minutes or until set.

For the Maple Currant Sauce

½ cup currants	½ cup Pinot Noir
¼ cup balsamic vinegar	2 cups chicken stock or low sodium canned broth
3 tablespoons butter	
2 large shallots, minced	¼ cup maple syrup

ADD currants to balsamic vinegar, let soak for half an hour. Place 1 tablespoon butter in a medium size saucepan over medium high, add shallots and cook until translucent, add balsamic, currants and Pinot Noir. Reduce by three-quarters and add chicken stock or broth. Reduce by half. Lower heat to a simmer and whisk in remaining butter. Adjust seasoning and keep warm for service.

Serves 4

Wine Pairing: Gloria Ferrer '01 Pinot Noir

The Molly Brown House and museum.

The Fort

The Fort

19192 Highway 8
Morrison, CO 80465
303-697-4771
www.thefort.com

January - March, Monday - Thursday
6:00 pm – 10:00 pm
Friday - Saturday 5:30 pm – 10:00 pm
Sunday 5:00 pm – 9:00 pm
April - December, Monday - Friday
5:30 pm - 10:00 pm
Saturday 5:00 pm - 10:00 pm
Sunday 5:00 pm - 9:00 pm

The Fort

Sam'l P. Arnold and Holly Arnold Kinney, Owners

Situated in Red Rock country, seventeen miles southwest of Denver on Highway 285, The Fort is a true replica of historic Bent's Fort...the first American community west of the Mississippi and rendezvous of Kit Carson and other mountain men.

Made with over 80,000 adobe bricks, along with beautiful hand-carved doors, beams and furniture in the Spanish Colonial tradition, The Fort has an early Western flavor. A huge 1840 bell hangs over the main gate and is rung to announce the meals. Above the bell tower flies a pre-Texas 27 star flag, the first American flag to fly over Colorado.

The nine dining rooms are white plastered-over adobe, and hanging Navajo rugs offer a bright contrast. Each table has a candle lamp.

The Cantina, or bar, has a huge Indian fireplace and cedar and pigskin chairs where you can relax and enjoy your cocktails Try their signature cocktail, The Hailstorm Mint Julep. Another interesting drink is Trade Whiskey - whiskey flavored with black gunpowder, tobacco, and red pepper. Cooking is done over open grills. There is also a separate smoke house that provides the smoke flavor for many dishes. The Fort is renown for their innovative specialties, such as superb young buffalo steaks, elk steaks, roasted quail, and fresh salmon. They have a special Gonzales steak (a large sirloin filled with green chili and Colorado-ranch beefsteaks). You must try the Rocky Mountain Oysters and Buffalo Marrow-Bones. In the summer you can have appetizers on the patio and watch the sun go down over the mountains and downtown Denver.

Sam'l P. Arnold and Holly Arnold Kinney

The Fort has a collection of historic art and a trade lodge that sells educational books and material about the early West. A visit to The Fort combines a sense of history with a terrific meal in one of Colorado's finest restaurants. The greatest joy for owners, Sam'l P. Arnold and his daughter, Holly Arnold Kinney, is to restore you with fine food, drink, and a warm hearty welcome.

JALAPENOS STUFFED WITH PEANUT BUTTER
appetizer

Lucy Delgado, well known in the 1960s as a traditionalist New Mexican cook, taught me to stuff peanut butter into peppers. "These are the best appetizers I know," she told me during one of our recipe swaps. "But if I show you how to make them, you have to promise to try them." Peanut butter–stuffed jalapenos! I vowed I would taste them even though they sounded stranger than a five-legged buffalo. She prepared some and said, as a last word of instruction, "Pop the entire pepper in to your mouth so you're not left with a mouthful of hot jalapeno and too little peanut butter." I gamely took the little morsel by the stem, and in it went. Miracle! Delicious!

Fearful of serving them to guests but eager to try them out on friends, I made them for my own parties until they became so popular that I put them on the menu. When NBC's Today Show came to Denver, Bryant Gumbel ate eight of them in a row. (Jane Pauley would have none of it.)   -Sam Arnold, founder, The Fort Restaurant

Ingredients

1 12-ounce can pickled jalapeno peppers
1½ cups peanut butter (smooth or chunky)

Preparation

SLICE the pickled jalapenos in half lengthwise not quite all the way through, leaving the 2 halves attached at the stem end. Using a knife or spoon, remove the seeds and ribs under running water. Pack the halves with peanut butter, press together, and arrange on a serving plate. Be sure to warn guests to put the whole pepper (except the stem) in the mouth before chewing, to get 70 percent peanut butter and 30 percent jalapeno. A nibbler squeezes out the peanut butter, changing the percentages and making it very hot indeed.

A FUN variation is to mix Major Grey's chutney with the peanut butter. It gives a nice fruity sweetness that also buffers the burn.

Serves 10 (2 per person, usually)

GONZALES STEAK

Ingredients

3 green Anaheim chilies, roasted, and peeled (canned will do, but fresh are best)
  salt
1 clove garlic, chopped
  pinch of Mexican leaf oregano

1 10-12 ounce thick-cut New York strip, top sirloin, or tenderloin of beef or buffalo steak
½ teaspoon salad oil
  freshly ground black pepper
1 teaspoon butter (optional)

Preparation

SLIT chilies to remove the seeds. Chop two chilies into fine dice and mix with the salt, garlic, and oregano. (New Mexicans traditionally like to leave a few of the seeds in the dish. The seeds give it life, they say.)

WITH a very sharp knife, cut a horizontal pocket into the steak. Stuff the chopped chilies into the pocket. Brush the meat and the remaining chili with salad oil. Grill the steak on both sides to the desired doneness. If using buffalo, watch carefully so as not to overcook. Because it contains less fat than chicken, bison cooks much faster than beef and is best medium-rare.

SALT and pepper the meat. Grill the remaining whole-roasted chili to get a nice patterning of grid burn on it. Lay it across the steak as a garnish.

A TEASPOON of brown butter on the steak as a special treat is heaven. To make brown butter, simply place the butter in a sauté pan over medium-high heat and allow it to melt and turn golden brown.

Serves 1

INCORRECT STEAK

Ingredients

New York strip steak, prepared
medium-rare
1 egg, fried, sunny side up

Dixon Red Chili Sauce (recipe follows)
Cabot (or other fine quality) white
cheddar cheese, grated

Preparation

TOP steak with a ladle of Dixon red chili sauce. Sprinkle with shredded cheddar cheese and top with fried egg. The heat from the sizzling steak, warm chili sauce, and egg will melt the cheese.

For the Dixon Red Chili Sauce

3 ounces canola or other vegetable oil
4 tablespoons flour
12 dried New Mexican red chilies, lightly
oven-toasted, stems broken off, and
seeds shaken out, or ½ cup pure New
Mexican red chili powder (medium to
mild; Medium Dixon is best)

1 clove garlic
½ teaspoon salt
½ teaspoon dry Mexican leaf oregano
½ cup hot water
½ teaspoon salt (unless broth is salted)
1 cup chicken broth (undiluted canned is
fine)

HEAT the oil in a sauté pan. Stir in the flour and cook to a golden brown.

TO MAKE red chili puree, place red chilies, garlic, salt, oregano, and hot water in a blender and zap into a smooth puree. Be sure to blend long enough to completely puree the garlic. The mixture should be loose and pourable. If necessary, add a bit more water.

ADD one cup red chili puree and salt to the oil and flour mixture and cook another 30 seconds, stirring constantly. Add the broth little by little, whisking it smooth. Add enough broth to make a medium-thin sauce.

Serves 1

Cinnamon-Chili Rubbed Buffalo Prime Rib

Ingredients

1 9-12 pound prime rib
Chili-Cinnamon rub (recipe follows)

Preparation

PREHEAT oven to 400 degrees.

GENEROUSLY rub bison meat with chili-cinnamon rub mixture.

WITH thermometer placed in the middle of prime rib, place meat in a preheated 400 degree oven on a sheet pan with a cooking rack on it (to keep the drippings off meat).

COOK for 15 minutes or so to sear outside of meat. Turn down the heat to 225 degrees and cook until the meat reaches an internal temperature of about 115 degrees. Let rest for 10-15 minutes before serving.

For the Chili-Cinnamon Rub

1 teaspoon kosher salt
1 tablespoon ground cinnamon
1½ tablespoons New Mexican chili powder (preferably Dixon)

3-4 turns of fresh ground black pepper
1 teaspoon sugar

MIX all dry ingredients together to form rub.

Serves 12

Teriyaki Quail

The West was built in good part by Chinese and Japanese immigrants who supplied both hands and brains to build railroads and cities, ranches and farms. Also, some of the first trappers who had been brought to our northwest coast by John Jacob Astor were Hawaiians. It is not surprising, therefore, that teriyaki came to the West early on.

Teriyaki Quail is accompanied by a grilled buffalo filet and elk medallion in The Fort's most popular entrée, The Game Plate. Lightly season the buffalo and elk with salt and pepper, then grill over an open flame to rare or medium rare. Following is the recipe for the teriyaki quail.

Ingredients

1 cup soy sauce
½ cup rice wine or dry sherry
¼ cup sugar
2 tablespoons minced fresh ginger
3 cloves garlic, minced
2 whole star anise

¼ cup orange peel, finely chopped
1 cup orange juice
1 cup water
8 2½ - 3½ ounce quail, partially deboned
4 orange slices for garnish

Preparation

COMBINE first nine ingredients in a saucepan and bring to a boil over high heat. Lower the heat and simmer for 5 minutes. Let cool.

PLACE the quail in a single layer in a pan, pour the marinade over, and let the quail marinate for 2 to 4 hours. Beware of leaving the birds in for more than 8 hours because the meat will become unpalatably salty.

WHEN ready to cook the quail, heat the grill to medium or preheat the broiler. Cook the quail for 3 to 4 minutes on each side. Garnish with a twisted orange slice.

Serves 8

NEGRITA

The negrita, or "little black one," originated in the Vera Cruz region of Mexico. While it bears a resemblance to chocolate mousse, its texture is very different. The negrita is firmer, like a slightly soft chocolate bar. Unlike many highly concentrated chocolate desserts, of which a few bites are enough, this one begs for the dish to be scraped (or licked) clean. A spoonful on the tip of the tongue followed by hot coffee is luscious. This recipe can be halved.

Ingredients

1¼	pounds Ghirardelli sweet dark chocolate (see note)	1	tablespoon vanilla extract
6	eggs	¼	cup rum
		½	pint heavy cream, whipped for topping

TO MELT the chocolate, place it in a double boiler over simmering water. Do not let the water touch the bottom of the bowl holding the chocolate. Stir the chocolate periodically. When it is about half melted, turn off the heat and leave it over the warm water to finish melting and to keep it warm.

SEPARATE the eggs. In a dry, clean bowl, beat the egg whites until stiff. In a separate bowl, beat the egg yolks until they're pale yellow.

CAREFULLY add the chocolate, vanilla, and rum to the egg yolks, then fold in the beaten whites. Stir until thoroughly blended. Ladle into 2½ ounce ramekins and chill. Serve topped with whipped cream.

NOTE: It is important not to let the chocolate cool too much before blending with the other ingredients, or it will become grainy. If you think it has become too cool by the time you're ready to use it, turn on the heat to warm it slightly.

Serves 10

Chef Jam

Chef Jam

1200 Miramonte Street
Broomfield, CO 80020
303-404-2525
www.chefjam.com

Thursday-Saturday
Check website for details

The Restaurant at ChefJam
James Mazzio, Executive Chef and Owner

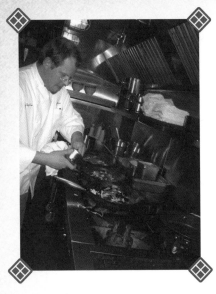

The Restaurant at ChefJam is a cozy candlelit eatery with an open kitchen and an innovative approach to the dining experience. The restaurant is located in a residential area of Broomfield. Among the many unique aspects of ChefJam is a completely open kitchen where you can view your entire meal being prepared, while you sip a full-bodied wine with your dinner companions. Each week, the menu changes and is available on the website for guests to consider which one of the intricate dishes they will choose on their arrival.

James Mazzio, Executive Chef and owner, has cooked in kitchens with world-renowned chefs and restaurateurs such as Daniel Boulud at Restaurant Daniel in New York, Thomas Keller at the French Laundry in Napa Valley, and the James Beard Foundation in New York. Hired as sous chef at Fifteen Degrees, Mazzio was soon promoted to head chef, winning the coveted title "Best New Chef 1999" from Food & Wine Magazine. Another successful restaurant venture followed: Triana restaurant, which opened to rave reviews from media and customers alike.

The next logical step for James was to open ChefJam Event Planning and Production. Originally intended only as a catered event planning and production facility, the space inspired Mazzio to create "The Restaurant at ChefJam". The ChefJam catering kitchen and dining room transforms into an award-winning restaurant on select nights of the week, including special guest appearances, wine tastings and theme nights.

Chef Mazzio was recently featured in The Denver Post as a "culinary cowboy", one of the "three maverick chefs drive(ing) western cuisine in new directions".

With a solid eclectic cooking foundation and a hard-earned self-confidence, Mazzio uses all of his talents at ChefJam and the restaurant at ChefJam, catering weddings, business luncheons, private dinners both big and small, and corporate team-building cooking classes.

The chef at work.

FRENCH GREEN LENTIL SOUP
with Portuguese Linguisa and Crawfish

This incredible combination of flavors elevates lentil soup to the sublime. This soup works well with any mild link sausage, like chorizo.

Ingredients

1 carrot	4-5 sprigs thyme, tied in a bundle
1 stalk celery	2 cups French green lentils, rinsed and
1 small onion	picked over
1 leek	6 cups water or stock
3 cloves garlic, peeled, blanched and	1 8-ounce package crawfish tails,
thinly sliced, vertically	cleaned and cooked
¾ tablespoon canola or other vegetable	1 8-ounce link linguisa, grilled and
oil	cubed
¼ tablespoon extra virgin olive oil	¼ cup parsley, chopped finely
salt to taste	drizzle extra virgin olive oil or squeeze
white pepper to taste	of lemon juice (optional)
2 bay leaves	

Preparation

FOR the mirepoix, dice carrot, celery, onion, and leek, add garlic and sauté. Heat a large stockpot over medium heat. Add canola and olive oil. Immediately add mirepoix, generous pinch of salt, white pepper, bay leaves, and thyme bundle. Sweat over medium heat until onions are translucent. Add lentils, stir to coat. Add water or stock. Bring to a boil, cover, and simmer until lentils are tender, approximately 30-45 minutes. Soup should be soupy, not thick. Season to taste.

TO SERVE, stir in crawfish and linguisa, or other mild sausage, just before serving. Sprinkle with parsley, drizzle with extra virgin olive oil or squeeze a little lemon juice on top.

Serves 8

BEST DAMN CAESAR SALAD EVER
with Shaved Parmigiano-Reggiano and White Anchovies

James' friend's mom made this for dinner one night and it was declared by all to be "The Best Damn Caesar Salad ever". In fact, James was so impressed he took the recipe with him to the Renaissance Hotel kitchen, where it soon replaced their old Caesar Salad recipe.

Ingredients

4 cloves garlic, peeled
1 tablespoon oil
   water for cooking, ice bath
1 tablespoon Dijon mustard
3 dashes Tabasco
2 dashes Worcestershire sauce
1 tablespoon Parmigiano-Reggiano, grated
3 anchovy fillets, drained from oil

juice of 2 lemons
2 egg yolks
2 cups oil
¼ cup red wine vinegar
   salt and white pepper
3 heads Romaine lettuce
   Parmigiano-Reggiano to garnish
16 white anchovy fillets, drained from oil
   Garlic Croutons (recipe follows)

Preparation

BOIL water and blanch garlic for one minute then put it in an ice bath. Drain, place garlic in a food processor, and pulse until coarsely chopped. Add small amount of oil, scrape down sides of food processor with a spatula. Pulse garlic again to combine oil. Reserve 1 tablespoon for crouton preparation.

TO MAKE dressing, place processed garlic, Dijon mustard, Tabasco, Worcestershire sauce, Parmigiano-Reggiano, anchovy fillets, lemon juice, and egg yolks in a food processor, process until smooth. Add oil, drizzling very gradually - dressing will thicken as it emulsifies. Add red wine vinegar to correct consistency. Season with salt and pepper.

WASH lettuce, spin dry and cut into segments across the rib.

TO SERVE, place Romaine lettuce in bowls. Garnish with croutons. Drizzle dressing over salad. Shave Parmigiano-Reggiano over each salad. Crisscross two white anchovies on top of each one.

For the Garlic Croutons

¼ cup oil blend (1 part extra virgin
  olive oil, 3 parts canola oil or other
  vegetable oil)
¼ cup butter, melted

1 tablespoon reserved garlic purée
2 tablespoons chopped parsley
6 cups bread, cubed

PREHEAT oven to 350 degrees. Whisk oil blend with butter, garlic, and parsley in a bowl. Toss bread cubes in oil blend to coat. Bake 10-15 minutes or until golden brown.

Serves 8

Chef Jam's busy kitchen.

ChefJam, Broomfield

GRILLED RIB-EYE STEAK
with Horseradish Aioli

This juicy, flavorful cut of beef, accented by fresh horseradish in a creamy aioli, reminds us that sometimes going back to the basics is best.

Ingredients

4 16-ounce rib-eye steaks, cut thick
1 tablespoon rosemary, chopped
1 tablespoon thyme, chopped
1 tablespoon garlic, blanched and chopped

½ tablespoon black pepper, coarsely ground
½ cup olive oil mixed with 1½ cup canola oil
    white and black peppercorns, crushed
    Horseradish Aioli (recipe follows)

Preparation

TO MAKE marinade, whisk rosemary, thyme, garlic, black pepper, and oil together. Refrigerate if not using immediately, then shake or whisk just before use.

WHEN ready to cook steaks, brush them with marinade, then season with salt and peppercorns and grill or broil to desired doneness in the center.

TO SERVE, add a dollop of horseradish aioli on each steak just before serving.

For the Horseradish Aioli

1½ cups canola oil or other vegetable oil
 ½ cup olive oil
 2 egg whites
 1 teaspoon Dijon mustard

salt and white pepper
juice of one lemon
1 teaspoon fresh rosemary
2 tablespoons horseradish

COMBINE canola and olive oil in a bowl and set aside. In a blender, blend all the other ingredients. Gradually drizzle in oil until emulsified. Refrigerate until ready to use.

Serves 4

Oven-Roasted Quail
with Blackcurrant-Bordelaise Sauce

A holiday favorite, James created this recipe to showcase how delicious quail can be.

Ingredients

4 large quail or Cornish game hens (2-5 ounces), European-style (boneless except for leg and wing)
kosher salt, pepper to taste
1 carrot
1 stalk celery
1 small onion
1 leek
3 cloves garlic, peeled and blanched (optional)
few sprigs fresh thyme
6 cups water
2 tablespoons oil blend (1 part extra virgin olive oil to 3 parts canola oil or other

vegetable oil)
¼ cup dried apricots, diced
¼ cup pine nuts, toasted
1 tablespoon fresh sage, chopped
salt and white pepper to taste
6 cups bread (such as focaccia, sourdough or other artisan bread), cubed
ChefJam Marinade (recipe follows)
Bordelaise Sauce (recipe follows)
Haricots Verts (recipe follows)

Preparation

PREHEAT oven to 400 degrees. Sauté finely diced carrot, celery, onion, leek, and garlic in butter to make mirepoix. Cut off quail wing tips, roast tips in oven until golden. Place tips in saucepan, add half of chopped mirepoix (reserving other half for stuffing), fresh thyme and water, bring to a boil, simmer until reduced to 4 cups of stock. Set aside half the stock (i.e. 2 cups) for sauce, half for stuffing.

PRE-HEAT a medium sauté pan on medium heat. Add oil blend, reserved brunoise mirepoix, apricots, nuts, and sage. Stir over medium heat until onions are translucent, but still al dente. Season. Add 2 cups of stock. Bring stock to a boil, re-season. Add bread cubes and stir. Mixture should be moist but not runny.

POUR into a baking sheet, cool in fridge until completely cold. Form stuffing into four balls. Open each quail by the legs, turning quail partially inside out. Place stuffing ball inside each quail, then reform quail right side out again. Cross quail legs and secure with toothpick. Rub quail with 2 tablespoons ChefJam marinade, salt generously. Roast quail 10-12 minutes in an ovenproof glass casserole dish lightly covered in oil.

OVEN-ROASTED QUAIL
with Blackcurrant-Bordelaise Sauce
CONTINUED

TO SERVE, place haricots verts in center of bowl or plate. Remove toothpick from quail, place quail in center of bowl. Pour bordelaise sauce over, straining out currants.

For the ChefJam Marinade

- 1 tablespoon rosemary, chopped
- 1 tablespoon thyme, chopped
- 1 tablespoon garlic, blanched and chopped

- ½ tablespoon black pepper, coarsely ground
- 2 cups oil blend (1 part extra virgin olive oil to 3 parts canola oil or other vegetable oil)

WHISK ingredients together. Refrigerate. Shake or whisk just before use.

For the Bordelaise Sauce

- 2 tablespoons dried blackcurrants, previously covered with port and rehydrated for at least 5 hours at room temperature

- 2 tablespoons veal demi-glace (see resource list)
- 2 cups reserved stock

HEAT sauté or sauce pan over medium heat. Add currants with the port, and demi-glace. Stir over medium heat until reduced. Add stock, bring to a boil, then remove from heat.

For the Haricots Verts

- 1 pound fresh haricots verts (or green beans)
- 1 tablespoons oil blend (1 part extra virgin olive oil to 3 parts canola oil or other

- vegetable oil)
- 1 teaspoon blanched garlic, chopped salt and pepper to taste

BLANCH haricots verts until al dente. Heat sauté pan over medium to high heat, add oil. Add beans to pan, toss with chopped garlic. Season to taste.

Serves 4

Manor House

The Manor House

1 Manor House Rd
Littleton, CO 80127
303-973-8064
www.themanorhouserestaurant.com

Tuesday –Friday
5:00 pm - 9:00 pm
Friday and Saturday
5:00 pm - 9:30 pm
Sunday
4:00 pm - 8:00 pm

The Manor House
Justin Wills, Executive Chef

The Manor House is one of Colorado's finest examples of a southern style American mansion. John Shaffer built the 8,000 square foot Manor House in 1914 for the sum of $100,000. The house was originally surrounded by the 28,000-acre Ken Caryl Cattle Ranch, which was named after his two sons, Kent and Carroll.

Shaffer was editor-publisher of the Chicago Tribune and then owner of the Chicago Post and Rocky Mountain News. He was a patron of the arts and spearheaded the fundraising to build Chicago's Opera House. Mr. Shaffer would engage opera companies to perform at the Denver Auditorium and would house the cast at the Manor House and ranch. There were 16 cottages on his acreage and the Manor House itself had six bedrooms and four baths.

Notable and frequent guests at the Manor House include Presidents Theodore Roosevelt and William Howard Taft, as well as industrial chieftains from around the world.

The 105-foot flagpole behind the restaurant has a light at the top that was originally battery operated. The light could be seen from Denver, through the saddle of the Dakota Hogback, and this was an invitation to Shaffer's friends to "come on out".

The Peterson Brothers opened this historic house as a restaurant in December 1990, taking care to preserve the original architecture of the historic structure. The New American Menu is the creation of Executive Chef Justin Wills, a graduate of The Culinary Institute of America in Hyde Park, New York.

Manor House, Littleton

118

GALIA MELON
with Lolla Rossa and Mizuna Greens

Ingredients

½ cup lolla rossa
½ cup mizuna
4 ¼-inch slices of Galia melon
3 tablespoons macadamia nuts, roasted,
   rough chopped

20 blood orange segments
⅛ cup Manchego cheese, shaved
   Ginger Vinaigrette (recipe follows)

Preparation

TO SERVE, place one slice of melon on each plate. Dress equal parts of lolla rossa and mizuna greens with 3/8 cup ginger vinaigrette. Place equal parts on top of each melon slice. Place five segments of blood orange on the edge of each melon slice. Shave Manchego cheese on top of the greens. Garnish with chopped macadamia nuts and the rest of the vinaigrette.

For the Ginger Vinaigrette

1 tablespoon ginger, fresh, peeled,
   grated
1 teaspoon granulated sugar
1 teaspoon Dijon mustard

⅓ cup unseasoned rice wine vinegar
1 cup olive oil
1 teaspoons kosher salt

COMBINE ginger, sugar, mustard, and rice wine vinegar in blender and blend on high speed until smooth. With blender on high, slowly drizzle olive oil into vinegar ginger mixture, until emulsified. Season with kosher salt. Reserve.

Serves 4

PASILLA CHILE AND COFFEE CRUSTED AHI TUNA
with Fermented Black Bean Sauce

Ingredients

4 3-ounce portions ahi tuna, center cut
   olive oil for cooking
   Pasilla Chile Coffee Crust
   (recipe follows)

Fermented Black Bean Sauce
(recipe follows)

Preparation

MAKE pasilla chile coffee crust and fermented black bean sauce, according to directions below. Coat ahi on all sides with crust. In a sauté pan, over medium heat, cook tuna on all sides in olive oil until the ahi is rare (white about ⅛" on all sides). Remove tuna from pan and slice thinly, against the grain (a serrated knife works well for this).

To serve, take four plates, sauce them with equal parts of the fermented black bean sauce, place thin slices of ahi on top of sauce and serve.

For the Pasilla Chile Coffee Crust

1 Pasilla chile, toasted, seeded and
   finely ground
1 tablespoon ground coffee
1 tablespoon coriander, toasted and
   ground

2 teaspoons thyme, dried
1 teaspoon kosher salt
½ teaspoon black pepper, coarse ground

COMBINE all ingredients. Reserve.

For the Fermented Black Bean Sauce

1 tablespoon ginger, chopped fine
1 tablespoon garlic, chopped fine
1 tablespoon scallion, thinly sliced,
   white part only

2 ounces fermented black beans, or
   Chinese black beans
1 ounce sherry
8 ounces veal stock
2 tablespoons soy sauce

SAUTÉ ginger, garlic, scallion, and black beans over medium-high heat.
Deglaze with sherry, and reduce until almost dry.
Add veal stock and reduce by half.
Season with soy sauce (use more or less depending on individual taste). Reserve.

Serves 4

PAN ROASTED HALIBUT
with Tomato Pot au Feu and Crispy Onions

Ingredients

4 6-ounces portions halibut
olive oil to cook

Tomato Pot au Feu (recipe follows)
Crispy Onion Rings (recipe follows)

Preparation

MAKE the tomato pot au feu and crispy onion rings.

PREHEAT oven to 400 degrees. Sauté halibut in olive oil over high heat in a smoking hot pan. Flip halibut and place in oven, cook to medium.

TO SERVE, take four bowls and ladle tomato pot au feu in equal parts into each bowl. Place cooked halibut on top and top with crispy onions. Enjoy!

For the Tomato Pot au Feu

2 ounces shallots, thinly sliced
1 ounce garlic, chopped
2 tablespoons butter, unsalted
10 ounces yellow pear tomatoes, halved
10 ounces red grape tomatoes, halved
¼ cup white wine

1½ cup chicken stock
1 tablespoon chives, thinly sliced
1 tablespoon basil, chopped
1 tablespoon thyme, fresh chopped
    salt and pepper to taste

IN A sauté pan sauté the shallots and garlic in butter until shallots are translucent. Add halved tomatoes and wine. Reduce until wine is evaporated. Add chicken stock and reduce by a third. Season with chopped herbs, salt, and pepper

For the Crispy Onion Rings

20 red onion rings, thinly sliced
    (⅛ inch)
1 cup buttermilk
2 cups all purpose flour

1 tablespoon ground coriander
2 teaspoons cayenne pepper
1 tablespoon salt
1 tablespoon pepper

COMBINE dry ingredients and reserve. Place sliced onion in buttermilk, and then place into seasoned flour. Fry in 375 degree olive oil until golden brown.

Serves 4

View of a family outing in Colorado. (1925)

Opus
Restaurant

Opus

2575 W. Main St.
Littleton, CO 80160
303-703-6787

Monday – Thursday
5:00 pm – 10:00 pm
Friday and Saturday
5:00 pm – 11:00 pm
Sunday Brunch
10:00 AM – 2:00 PM

Chef Michael Long.

Opus Restaurant
Michael Long, Chef

In the dictionary, the word "opus" is defined as a creative piece of work in any field of the arts, and it's clear that Chef Michael Long takes his role seriously, combining the symphony of textures and flavors into meals both delightful and unforgettable.

The Opus Restaurant is located in old Littleton, a quaint little town that retains much of its turn-of-the-century charm. The restaurant itself is housed in a 114-year-old building, and the interior strikes a pleasing balance between friendly ambiance and personal space.

The walls are painted a rich mustard color and decorated with colorful artwork. A stacked stone fireplace divides the restaurant and the pastry café area, and the tables are cozy but allow enough space to walk around comfortably. Echoing the musical Opus theme, the open kitchen at one end of the room is framed by red curtains, which are pulled closed with a flourish at the end of the evening.

Chef Michael Long is a graduate of the Culinary Institute of America 1991, and he honed his skills at several top Florida and east coast establishments. Returning to Colorado, he and his partners opened up the 5280 Roadhouse and Brewery in the 104-year-old mill downtown, then Long opened Opus Restaurant in August 2002. The cuisine at Opus is contemporary New American, and dishes include elements of Mediterranean, Asian, Creole, and Southwestern cooking in a creative and innovative presentation.

Opus Restaurant has been recognized by the Rocky Mountain News, receiving a Four-Star rating, and the comment: "impeccable service". 5280 Magazine stated Opus offered "the best meal you'll eat in a long time". WestWord Magazine selected the restaurant for the Best of WestWord 2004- Best special events menu, with the quote, "genius on a plate".

A visit to Opus Restaurant is truly a performance not to be missed.

Opus dining area.

COLORADO PEACH BISQUE
with Amaretto, Spiced Almonds, and Haystack Farms Goat Cheese

Ingredients

12 large ripe Colorado peaches
 4 each shallots, minced
 2 ribs celery
 3 tablespoons butter
 ¼ cup rice flour
 ½ cup Half & Half
    pinch of bay seasoning

    salt
    pepper
 2 tablespoons Amaretto
    Spiced Almonds (recipe follows)
    Goat Cheese Rounds (recipe follows)
    thin croutons (optional)

Preparation

IN A medium non-reactive saucepan, sauté peaches and vegetables in butter until softened. Add rice flour and cook briefly. Add Half & Half, and seasoning. Bring to a slow boil, reduce heat and simmer gently for 10 minutes. Remove from heat, add Amaretto and puree. Strain and hold warm.

TO SERVE, place warm soup in large bowls. Gently float goat cheese rounds on top. Garnish with thin croutons and spiced almonds.

For the Spiced Almonds

24 whole almonds
 1 teaspoon brown sugar
 1 teaspoon cayenne pepper

 1 teaspoon celery salt
 1 teaspoon nutmeg, grated fresh
 1 ounce butter, melted

Combine all. Toast in a 350 degree oven 10 minutes.

For the Goat Cheese Rounds

 8 ounce log Haystack Farms Goat Cheese
 ¼ cup chives, chopped

ROLL goat cheese in chives. Slice into four rounds, reserve.

Serves 4

SUNKIST SHRIMP "SUNBURST"
with Citrus Mojo, Plantain Stuffing and Avocado-Grapefruit Relish

Ingredients

60 jumbo shrimp (under 12 per pound)
kosher salt
freshly ground pepper
zest from 8 navel oranges and limes,
very finely minced

Plantain Stuffing (recipe follows)
Avocado-Grapefruit Relish
(recipe follows)
Citrus Mojo (recipe follows)

Preparation

MAKE the plantain stuffing, avocado-grapefruit relish, and citrus mojo according to directions below.

PEEL and devein the shrimp, leaving very end of tail on. Reserve the shells. Butterfly the shrimp, but do not split through. Lightly flatten each shrimp. Season the shrimp with salt, pepper, and citrus zest. Place a tablespoon of stuffing in the center of each shrimp.

PLACE stuffed shrimp in a 400 degree oven for 10-12 minutes or until just cooked through. While shrimp is cooking, place ½ cup of citrus mojo sauce in the center of the serving plate and let pool. Arrange reserved citrus sections around sauce in "sunburst" pattern. Place avocado relish in the center of plate. Remove shrimp from oven and place five on each plate, with tails facing out, following the "sunburst" pattern. Or place fried decorative chips from one thin sliced green plantain over avocado relish.

For the Plantain Stuffing

3 semi-ripe plantains, small diced
4 tablespoons olive oil
½ cup small onion, diced
¼ cup small red bell pepper, diced
1 teaspoon serrano chili, minced

¼ cup small celery, diced
3 cups raw spinach, packed, sliced
2 tablespoons raisins, soaked in 1
tablespoon banana liqueur

HEAT olive oil in a large sauté pan. Add onions, peppers, and celery. Cook until softened, then add plantains. Lower heat and cook for 8-10 minutes or until plantains are cooked. Add spinach and raisins (with liquid). Spinach should wilt and moisten the stuffing, Remove from heat and reserve.

For the Citrus Mojo

12 navel oranges (including zested ones)
6 grapefruit
12 limes (including zested ones)
  shrimp shells
4 cups mild fish stock
4 tablespoons olive oil
2 cups onion, very fine diced
1 serrano chili, minced

4 tablespoons garlic, minced
1 tablespoon cracked black peppercorns
1 cup spiced rum
4 tablespoons white wine vinegar
1 tablespoon cornstarch, dissolved in 2
  tablespoons water
2 bunches cilantro, roughly chopped
4 scallions, sliced very thin

PEEL and section six oranges and all grapefruit. Reserve the sections. Squeeze all juice from remainder of citrus. Toast the shrimp shells until pink and simmer in the stock for 20 minutes, then strain. In a heavy saucepan, heat the olive oil until very hot, then add onion, chili, garlic, and peppercorns. Cook until soft, and then add rum and vinegar. Reduce by half, then add citrus juice. Simmer, and thicken with cornstarch. Add cilantro and scallions, remove from heat, hold warm.

For the Avocado Grapefruit Relish

6 each ripe avocados, large diced
3 grapefruit, sectioned
1 clove garlic, smashed into a paste
½ cup red onion, finely minced
2 tablespoons chopped fresh mint

  juice from one lime
2 tablespoons extra-virgin olive oil
  kosher salt to taste
  fresh ground pepper to taste
  crushed cumin seed to taste

GENTLY mix all ingredients and set aside until needed.

Serves 12

BRAISED SALMON "OSSO BUCO"

This dish does not bear any relation to traditional Osso Buco, but is meant to recreate that presentation. "Osso Buco " means "bone with a hole" and this entrée has both.

Ingredients

4 6-ounce salmon fillet pieces	1 large garlic clove, sliced
4 medium parsnips, middle section carved to look like bone, and hollowed on top (reserve all trimmings for use below)	1 large pinch saffron
	½ Italian plum tomato, crushed
	1 cup shrimp stock (made with shrimp shells)
4 long strips from 1 washed leek, remainder sliced, washed and reserved for the sauce	12 each large shrimp, peeled and deveined
2 tablespoons extra virgin olive oil	½ cup dry white wine
4 ounces carrot, diced	1½ ounces cornstarch
4 ounces celery, diced	2 tablespoons Italian parsley for garnish
4 ounces parsnip trimmings, diced	2 tablespoons fresh basil for garnish
4 ounces leek remainder, diced	Gnocchi (recipe follows)
	Gremolata (recipe follows)

Preparation

BUTTERFLY salmon filets and tie them with the long strips from the leek

IN THE one pot, sear the salmon, add carrot, celery, parsnip, leek, garlic, saffron, tomato, shrimp stock, shrimp, wine and cornstarch, in order listed. Remove salmon to steamer top, add gnocchi, and cook until sauce is thickened. Place parsnip bones in center of fillet pieces prior to service, and add gremolata to hollow spot. Ladle gnocchi and sauce around, garnish with fresh basil and parsley in small edible pieces.

For the Gnocchi

1 cup ricotta cheese	coarse salt
2 eggs, beaten	fresh ground pepper
½ cup semolina flour	10 fresh basil leaves, chiffonade
1 cup all purpose flour	

COMBINE cheese and beaten eggs. Gently mix in flours, salt and pepper to taste. Let dough rest in a cool place. When rested, cut and add basil. Roll, cut, cover, reserve. There will be more dough than needed for four servings.

For the Gremolata

      zest of two oranges   *salt*
2-3 *cloves garlic, crushed*   *extra virgin olive oil (about two*
  ½ *cup picked Italian parsley leaves*   *tablespoons)*

ALTERNATE chopping and crushing first three ingredients together. Add oil slowly and carefully, salt to taste. Reserve.

Serves 4

COLORADO LAMB DUO
Goat Cheese and Corn Crusted Lamb Rack, with Lamb Shank Arepas, and Merlot Mole Sauce

This excellent dish is garnished with chive oil, red pepper oil, and fried tomatillos. Tortilla strips can be used to replicate rack bones.

Ingredients

- 1 quarter rack of Colorado lamb, trimmed, frenched
- 4 ounces Haystack Farms Goat Cheese
- 1 tablespoon sage, chiffonade
- 4 ounces crushed dried corn kernels (not all will be used)

Lamb Shank and Mole Base (recipe follows)
Arepas (recipe follows)
zucchini and red peppers for two (recipe follows)

SEASON the lamb rack with coarse salt and fresh pepper. Sear rack in an iron skillet or very hot grill until rare. Cool and remove bones to flavor stock. Coat rack with remaining ingredients, with the corn being last. Reserve until ready to serve. Prepare the base, arepas and vegetables.

Roast lamb rack in oven until medium rare

TO SERVE, place warm arepas in center of plate, ladle sauce around. Arrange vegetables, remove rack from oven slice and place on sauce.

For the Lamb Shank and Mole Base

- 1 16-ounce (with bone) Colorado lamb shank, trimmed and seasoned
- 2 tablespoons peanut oil
- 6 large tomatillos (4 peeled and diced, two reserved for garnish)
- 1 poblano pepper, diced
- ½ Spanish onion, diced
- 1 clove garlic, crushed
- 1 ancho chili, toasted, seeds removed, diced

- 2 tablespoons toasted pumpkin seeds
- 1 cup rich lamb stock or demi glace flavored with lamb rack bones
- 2 cups Plum Creek merlot
- 2 ounces bittersweet chocolate
- 1 teaspoon cumin seed
- 1 pinch cayenne
  salt to taste

SEAR lamb shank in a heavy-duty small braising pan, using peanut oil. Remove and add all vegetable ingredients and pumpkin seeds. Sweat on high heat until caramelization begins to occur. Deglaze with liquids, add chocolate and seasonings – do not over season – sauce will be highly reduced later!

RETURN shank to pot and bring to a steady simmer - cover tightly and place in 300 degree oven for 4 hours or until meat is fork tender. Cool meat in stock, remove shank, and all fat from surface of liquid. Pull lamb meat from bone and reserve. Puree stock, strain and reduce by ¾. Reserve all and keep warm.

For the Arepas

    1½ cups milk
     2 tablespoon butter
     2 ears corn, kernels cut off cob (cob
        scraped into milk)
    ¾   cup fine cornmeal (adjust by eye)
        salt and pepper to taste

     1 egg, beaten
     2 scallions, sliced very thin
   2-4 ounces cooked lamb shank meat
     4 ounces queso blanco cheese or
        mixture of cheddar and jack cheeses

BRING milk, butter, and corn to a boil in a small saucepan. Slowly add the cornmeal in slow steady stream until mixture is thick like polenta. Salt and pepper to taste. Remove from heat and add egg and scallions. Chill, cut into 4 disks and reserve. Mix lamb shank meat with cheese. Layer between arepas cakes and heat slowly on griddle. Place in oven to heat through.

For the Vegetables

     2 zucchini
     2 red peppers

CUT zucchini and red peppers in decorative arrows. Blanch and sauté briefly in whole butter. Season.

Serves 2

Wine suggestion: Plum Creek Merlot

VANILLA MAPLE GLAZED DUCK BREAST
with Pecan Butternut Stuffed Duck Leg, Mustard Greens and Spice Grilled Peaches

Ingredients

3 5-6 pound Maple Leaf ducklings
course salt to taste
freshly ground pepper to taste
oil for cooking
Vanilla Maple Glaze (recipe follows)

Pecan Butternut Squash Stuffed Duck
Legs (recipe follows)
Mustard Greens (recipe follows)
Spice Grilled Peaches (recipe follows)
toasted pecans for garnish

Preparation

BONE the ducklings. Separate the breasts, trim them, and lightly score the skin. Remove the cartilage at the end of each leg. Remove each thighbone, and loosen the drumstick bone. Gently pull the drumstick bone so that it leaves a cavity in the leg - do not remove it. Lightly flatten the thigh with a mallet, so the meat is of an even thickness. Remove as much fat from bones as is possible. Reserve giblets and fat for another use. Chop the bones of one carcass as small as possible. Chill breasts and legs while starting the rest of this recipe.

PREPARE vanilla maple glaze, pecan butternut squash stuffed duck legs, mustard greens, spice grilled peaches according to recipes below.

WHEN ready to serve, season the duck breasts with coarse salt and freshly ground pepper. Sear them, skin down in a hot skillet. Turn the breasts and sauté until they are pink throughout and skin is mostly rendered. Keep warm.

PUT the stuffed duck legs under a broiler until skin crisps. Remove foil and toothpicks. Place sautéed mustard greens in the center of each plate. Place legs over mustard greens. Ladle glaze over duck legs, slice breast into three pieces each, and plate around legs. Garnish with grilled peaches and toasted pecans.

For the Vanilla Maple Glaze
(not all of this glaze is needed for 6 servings)

chopped duck bones
4 shallots, minced
2 large fresh vanilla beans, split
¼ cup red wine vinegar
2 cups pure maple syrup, of highest
    quality

1 cup soy sauce
1 tablespoon cracked fresh pepper
2 cups water or duck stock (stock is
    preferred)

HEAT a heavy bottomed saucepan until very hot. Sear the duck bones until browned, add shallots and vanilla bean, deglaze with vinegar, then add remaining ingredients. Bring to a boil, and simmer one hour, skimming occasionally. Strain. Glaze should be thick enough to coat the back of a spoon. If it is not, reduce as necessary.

For the Pecan Butternut Squash Stuffed Duck Legs

½ cup each onion and celery, very finely diced
1 medium size butternut squash, cut into small dice
¾ cup toasted pecan pieces

½ cup fresh bread crumbs
1 tablespoon fresh sage, sliced
3 tablespoons butter
coarse salt
ground pepper

SAUTÉ the onions and celery in butter until translucent. Add butternut squash, pecans, and bread crumbs and mix completely. Season and place pan with stuffing into a 350 degree oven. Bake for twenty minutes, then remove and mix in sage. Cool stuffing. When cool enough, place stuffing into duck leg cavities, and press firmly. Pull bone mostly out, and press stuffing in to fill legs completely. Shape legs into a round "pear" shape. Secure open end of thigh with toothpicks. Turn oven up to 425 degrees and prick skin all over on duck legs. Cover exposed bone with foil to prevent burning. Season the legs with salt and pepper and then roast for 35 minutes. Hold in a warm place.

For the Mustard Greens

1½ pounds fresh mustard greens, washed
1 gallon salted water
4 ounces duck fat

olive oil to taste
salt and pepper to taste

BRING one gallon of salted water and duck fat to a rolling boil. Blanch mustard greens until fully cooked. Shock in ice water. Just prior to serving sauté the greens in olive oil, salt, and pepper.

For the Spice Grilled Peaches

4 large ripe peaches, peeled, pitted, and cut into wedges
1 teaspoon cayenne pepper
1 teaspoon fresh ground black pepper

1 teaspoon grated fresh nutmeg
1 teaspoon coarse salt
1 teaspoon cinnamon
2 tablespoons extra virgin olive oil

COMBINE all seasonings in a metal bowl. Add peaches and coat with spices. Grill them on each side until just beginning to soften. Remove from grill and reserve.

Serves 6

Hazelnut Chocolate Sundial Tart
with Peach Sauce and Peach Custard

Ingredients

2½ cups all-purpose flour
2 teaspoons cinnamon
2 sticks cold butter, cut into small pieces
½ cup sugar
1 teaspoon salt
2 egg yolks (reserve egg whites)

Hazelnut Chocolate Filling
(recipe follows)
Peach Custard (recipe follows)
Creekside Moscato Peach Sauce
(recipe follows)
Chocolate Sauce (recipe follows)

Preparation

MAKE the hazelnut chocolate filling, the peach custard, the peach sauce, and chocolate sauce.

TO MAKE crust, add flour and cinnamon to bowl of a food processor. Process, pulsing while slowly adding the small pieces of butter. Transfer mix to mixing bowl and gently add sugar, salt and egg yolks. Add more flour if dough is too sticky to pull away from bowl. Knead gently into a ball and let rest, refrigerated, at least 2 hours.

PLACE dough on floured surface, divide in half and roll each out about 1/4 inch thickness. Grease and lightly flour two 8-inch tart pans. Place each half of dough half in its own pan and press down gently, shearing any overlap off with a rolling pin. Bake at 350 degrees for twenty minutes. Remove to a cool place and reserve.

TO SERVE, take 12 large white plates and use chocolate sauce to pipe Roman Numerals in a clockwise formation. Slice room temperature tarts into 12 equal pieces, and place one on each plate, at right angles. Drizzle peach sauce onto plates in an attractive pattern. Remove custard from molds or spoon out and place adjacent to tarts. If desired, using a triangle stencil, dust the plate with cocoa powder to resemble the shadow cast by the tart, making sure to have it indicate the same time as the time that the tart is being served.

For the Hazelnut Chocolate Filling

8 ounces bittersweet chocolate
½ stick cold butter
½ cup sugar
2 eggs plus two egg whites
    (use reserved egg whites)

⅔ cup corn syrup
2 cups peeled, toasted hazelnuts (lightly
    crushed, with many still whole)

TO MAKE the filling, melt chocolate and butter together in a mixing bowl over a double boiler, stirring to blend well. In another bowl, whisk eggs, whites, sugar, and corn syrup. Remove chocolate from heat and stir in egg mixture, and then add toasted hazelnuts. Pour chocolate hazelnut filling into cooled tart shells and return to 350 degree oven. Bake for 40 minutes, or until center is completely set. Cool finished tarts at room temperature on a rack.

For the Peach Custard

3 each ripe peaches, peeled, pitted and diced
½ cup tablespoons heavy cream

4 egg yolks
¼ cup sugar

DICE the peaches very small. Simmer in cream until reduced to one cup. Puree, strain. Whisk the egg yolks very well with sugar, add mixture to peach cream, and pour into ceramic ramekins. Bake at 300 degrees in a water bath until custards are firmly set, about 2 hours in 6-ounce ramekins. Chill. Remove custard with a spoon and place in chocolate cups if desired, or hold in ramekins until time to serve.

For the Creekside Moscato Peach Sauce

6 each large peaches, peeled and pitted, quartered
½ cup sugar

2 tablespoons butter
1 vanilla bean, split
½ cup Creekside Cellars Moscato

WARM butter and sugar together in a small pan. Add peaches, vanilla, and wine. Bring to a simmer, and cook until peaches are soft. Chill completely then puree and strain.

For the Chocolate Sauce (this makes extra-it stores very well)

½ pound bittersweet chocolate
¼ cup corn syrup

MELT chocolate over a double boiler. When melted, add warm corn syrup. Cool to room temperature, place in a small parchment piping.

Serves 12

The camp feast, near Norrie, Colorado. (between 1900 and 1919)

Restaurant Kody

restaurant**kody**

1552 Bergen Parkway #102   Tuesday - Saturday
Evergreen, Colorado 80439   5:30 pm until closing
303-670-2263
www.restaurantkody.com

Restaurant Kody
Adam Mali, Chef

Restaurant Kody is located in a large red historical barn in the foothills of Evergreen. Named for their golden retriever, Kody, the restaurant is very much a collaborative effort for Mary and Adam Mali. They took their experience at award-winning restaurants from the East Coast to Arizona and San Francisco, and put it all into creating Restaurant Kody.

Chef Adam Mali began cooking professionally in New York City in 1983, right after high school.

Adam wanted to start a restaurant of his own, and he missed living in the mountains, so in 2002, he relocated to Colorado. His high school sweetheart, Mary Song, soon to be his wife, joined him there and they began their search for the perfect location.

It was Chef Mali's stepfather who suggested they look into possible space at the historic Hiwan Barn. It seemed like a long shot, but is also looked like the perfect location.

There was space available and the Malis found a home for Restaurant Kody, an intimate, warm, and elegant 40-seat restaurant.

The Malis worked together to renovate the space, creating an atmosphere with hints of the Mediterranean in this rustic mountain location. Mary handles the front of the house while her husband creates the regionally inspired dishes.

Chef Adam uses only the freshest quality ingredients for his menu, which changes daily, and everything is made on-site, from breads and soups to entrees and desserts. The wine list constantly changes to complement the menu, and the restaurant also has top shelf liquors and after dinner drinks.

Mary greets the guests with warmth, friendliness, and grace, making guests feel comfortable and pampered.

The combination is unbeatable, as evidenced by Restaurant Kody's inclusion in the Top Ten Restaurants in Denver 2003 compiled by 5280 Magazine.

Restaurant Kody, Evergreen

138

Roasted Butternut Squash Soup
with Sage Crème Fraîche

Ingredients

2 large butternut squash
4 teaspoons pure olive oil,
   (not extra virgin)
   kosher salt
   white pepper
½ teaspoon fresh thyme, chopped
1 medium yellow onion
1 cup sherry
1 cup white wine

1 teaspoon sherry vinegar
1½ quarts duck stock, chicken stock, or
   broth
½ cup pure maple syrup
2 teaspoons fresh sage (roughly
   chopped, to be strained later)
1 teaspoon ground cloves
1 teaspoon cinnamon
   Crème Fraîche (recipe follows)

Preparation

CUT squash vertically, and rub with olive oil, salt, pepper, and thyme. Roast at 325 degrees until tender, and slightly brown on surface, but not burned. Cool, and scoop flesh into a bowl.

SWEAT onion in olive oil, allowing minimal caramelization. Add roasted squash. Deglaze with sherry, let alcohol cook out, add white wine, and again, let the alcohol cook out. Add vinegar. Next add hot stock, simmer for about 30 minutes. Add maple syrup, sage, cloves, and cinnamon. Simmer for another 10 minutes. Add salt and pepper to adjust seasoning. Salt will bring out the sweetness to a point, and after that, it will only add saltiness.

PICK out as much of the sage as you can. Cool soup. To adjust consistency, puree in mixer until smooth. If it needs thinning, add heavy cream. If it needs to be thickened, cook down some more.

SERVE soup with a dollop of crème fraîche as garnish.

For the Crème Fraîche

1 pint creme fraîche, or sour cream
1 lemon, if sour cream is used

1 teaspoon sage, minced finely
   salt to taste

ADD all ingredients together, set aside until needed.

Serves 4-6

Wine Pairing: Acacia Chardonnay, Carneros

SAUTÉED MUSSELS, TOMATO-FENNEL COMPOTE
with White Wine Saffron Broth

Ingredients

15	mussels, cleaned and de-bearded
2-4	strands saffron
8	ounces white wine, such as Pouilly-Fumé
1	tablespoon garlic, finely minced
2	ounces fennel, small to medium dice

	fish stock or clam juice to cover
1	Roma tomato, seeded, diced
	salt and pepper to taste
1	teaspoon parsley, finely minced
1	tablespoon scallion, cut on bias, chiffonade

Preparation

STEEP all but one saffron strand in simmering white wine to change color to gold. Sauté garlic in olive, add mussels, and coat with oil and garlic. Add fennel, cook until soft. Deglaze with wine and reduce slightly. Add saffron and fish stock or clam juice to cover; cook until mussels are mostly opened. Add tomato, toss, season, and add parsley. To serve, place the tomato-fennel compote in center of the plate, with mussels around the rim. Garnish with scallion.

Serves 1

GRILLED LAMB SPARERIBS
with Lavender Honey

Ingredients

4 *pounds Denver ribs, or lamb spareribs*	¼ *cup fresh rosemary, chopped*
2 *teaspoons olive oil*	¼ *cup fresh mint, rough chopped*
1 *carrot, peeled and chopped*	4 *cloves garlic*
1 *celery stick, chopped*	1 *teaspoon peppercorn*
1 *yellow onion, diced*	1 *each bay leaf*
1 *cup red wine*	1 *cup wildflower honey*
2 *cups beef broth*	1 *teaspoon ground lavender*
	salt to taste

Preparation

BROWN lamb ribs well in olive oil. Drain fat. Remove lamb from roasting pan and reserve. Cook carrot, celery, and onion until well caramelized. Add red wine, and let reduce by one-third. Add beef broth or stock, and put lamb ribs back in. Bring up to a boil.

ADD rosemary, mint, garlic, peppercorns, bay leaf, one-half the honey, and one-half the ground lavender. Cover with foil, and bake at 350 degrees for 3-4 hours. Check liquid level regularly, add more stock if it is too low.

MIX remaining honey and lavender, and reserve. Remove from oven, and reserve lamb. Strain the liquid from the roasting pan, and cool. The lamb fat should rise to the top, and should be skimmed off.

HEAT remaining liquid, and add salt to taste, hold.

BRUSH honey-lavender mixture on the lamb ribs, and grill until marked. Pour sauce over and serve.

Serves 6-8

Wine Pairing: Robert Sinskey Pinot Noir

CHOCOLATE-LAVENDER TART
with Vanilla Caramel Sauce

Ingredients

12 ounces bittersweet chocolate
(preferably Scharffenberger)
2 tablespoons ground lavender petals
1 cup heavy cream

Tart Shell (recipe follows)
Vanilla-Caramel Sauce
(recipe follows)
cocoa powder for garnish

Preparation

TO MAKE filling, chop chocolate into small bits. Add lavender to cream. Boil heavy cream infused with lavender. Strain and pour mixture over chocolate, and let stand for 2 minutes. Mix with spatula until smooth, uniform consistency.

MAKE tart shell and vanilla-caramel sauce. To assemble, unmold shell, and pour mixture into shell, smoothing with a spatula so that surface looks like an ice skating pond. Refrigerate immediately, cover with plastic wrap. Right before serving, warm the vanilla caramel sauce, spoon over top and sift cocoa powder to garnish.

For the Tart Shell

½ cup butter
½ cup sugar
¾ teaspoon vanilla extract

⅓ cup sifted, unsweetened cocoa powder
1 cup flour

CREAM butter, sugar, and vanilla. Add cocoa powder, incorporate well. Add flour and mix. Put mixture in plastic wrap, and form it into a ball. Let rest in refrigerator for about ½ hour. Form into tart pan, trim excess, and bake at 350 degrees until edges harden slightly. Cool completely.

For the Vanilla-Caramel Sauce

1 cup sugar
¼ teaspoon vanilla extract

4 ounces butter
¼ cup heavy cream

CARAMELIZE sugar completely, being careful to not burn it. Add vanilla, and stir. Add butter and cream, stir until uniform consistency. Cool and refrigerate if not used immediately.

Serves 1

Wine Pairing: Warre's Otima, 10 year old Tawny Port

Briarwood Inn

The
BRIARWOOD
Inn

1630 8th St.
Golden, CO 80401
303-279-3121
www.thebriarwoodinn.com

Lunch Monday – Friday
11:00 am – 2:00 pm
Dinner Monday - Sunday
5:00 pm – 9:00 pm
Sunday Brunch
10:30 am – 2:30 pm

The Briarwood Inn

J ust a half-hour drive from Denver puts you in the foothills of the Rocky Mountains, in the lovely town of Golden. As you step out of your car at the entrance of The Briarwood Inn, you will revel in the crisp pine-scented mountain air.

The Briarwood Inn was built in the mid-60's and has a rustic look from the exterior. But, step inside to experience a luxurious setting for fine dining. There are three distinct dining rooms, each furnished with American and European antiques. The high ceilings are adorned with heavy wood beams and elegant chandeliers. Ornate wood paneling and large oak-trimmed mirrors complete the luxurious décor. Of course, in such a setting, one expects the dinner service to equal the décor. The diner is treated to fine crystal and hand-painted china on colorful linens.

The Briarwood Inn has maintained an excellent reputation for fine food and wines for many years, winning the Mobil Travel Guide Four Star Award, along with the Wine Spectator Award of Excellence.

Executive Chef Tom Morris has assembled a tempting menu featuring Colorado beef along with a wide variety of seafood, including Rocky Mountain rainbow trout and King salmon. Game dishes also enhance the menu, including Elk Medallions finished with natural reduction flavored with raspberry and port wine. But, before you choose your entrée, enjoy the appetizer tray that includes fresh gulf shrimp, duck and chicken liver paté, and smoked salmon butter to spread on toast or crackers.

For a special Sunday treat, take a leisurely drive to The Briarwood Inn for their Sunday Brunch. A glass of Champagne, fresh seasonal fruits and an assortment of freshly baked pastries accompany your choice of tempting brunch fare. Try the Eggs Columbia, fresh Norwegian King salmon poached in white wine and served in a pastry with asparagus cream sauce, then topped with a poached egg laced with fresh dill butter. The signature Prime Benedict combines Prime Rib and Eggs Benedict to insure that you do not leave hungry.

The extensive award winning wine list contains more than 700 vintages from around the world. Wines are suggested for each entrée, and the knowledgeable staff is always ready to assist you in choosing just the right compliment for your dinner.

SMOKED SALMON BUTTER

This is delicious on imported crackers or toast points. Other hot smoked fish can be used, if desired.

Ingredients

½ pound hot smoked salmon
⅛ teaspoon Tabasco sauce
1 pound softened, lightly salted butter

1 teaspoon Worcestershire sauce
1 teaspoon finely minced shallots
¼ teaspoon liquid smoke (optional)

Preparation

BONE and skin smoked salmon. Combine all other ingredients in mixer and blend for two minutes. Break up salmon and add to mixture, mix for one additional minute, then serve.

Makes about 1½ cups.

The Briarwood's dining room.

Cioppino

Ingredients

4 tablespoons butter
2 tablespoons flour
1 small onion, medium diced
½ green bell pepper, julienned
⅓ pound button mushrooms, halved
1½ teaspoon kosher salt
2 tablespoons fresh oregano, finely chopped
2 tablespoons fresh basil, finely chopped
   pinch of rubbed sage
⅛ teaspoon thyme
2 teaspoons garlic, finely minced
1½ cups V-8 juice
1 14-ounce can whole pear tomatoes

2 tablespoons Worcestershire sauce
½ cup Chablis
1 cup clam juice
8 cherry stone clams, washed
8 greenlip mussels, bearded and washed
8 jumbo sea scallops
½ pound bay scallops
½ pound small gulf shrimp, peeled, and deveined
4 snow crab claws
¼ pound swordfish, cubed
½ zucchini, wedged
¼ cup whole black pitted olives

Preparation

MELT two tablespoons butter in a small saucepan, whisk in flour until smooth, and cook for 3-4 minutes to make the roux. Set aside.

IN A large saucepan, melt two tablespoons of butter and sauté onions, peppers, mushrooms, and spices until onions are soft. Add V-8 juice, whole pear tomatoes, Worcestershire sauce, wine, and clam juice, then bring to a boil.

STIR in roux. Reduce heat, add seafood, zucchini, and black olives, bring back to a boil for 1-3 minutes and serve immediately.

Serves 4-8

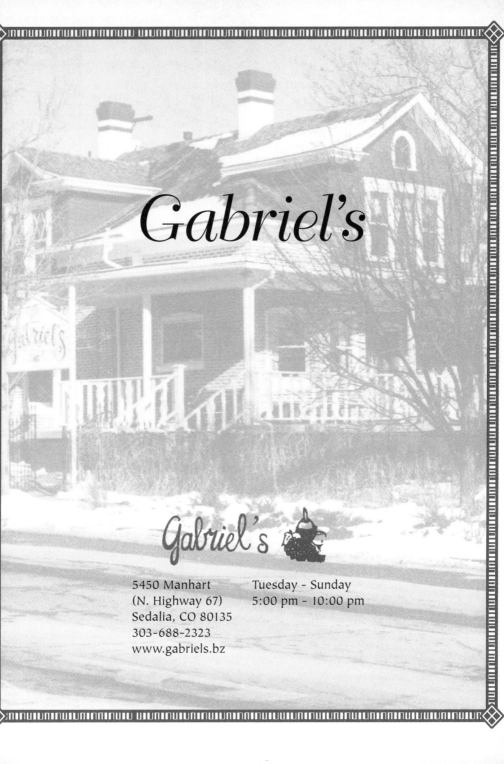

Gabriel's

5450 Manhart
(N. Highway 67)
Sedalia, CO 80135
303-688-2323
www.gabriels.bz

Tuesday - Sunday
5:00 pm - 10:00 pm

Gabriel's
Matthew and Jan Bundy, Owners
Tony Sanabria, Executive Chef

Gabriel's, a Colorado tradition since 1985, is locally owned and operated by Matthew and Jan Bundy. The northern Italian restaurant is located in a Victorian home, built in 1889 by the Manharts, a pioneer mercantile family. The Manhart home passed from generation to generation until 1978, when it was sold and became Mr. K's French Restaurant, then ultimately Gabriel's.

The atmosphere is elegant and upscale. The romantic and intimate dining rooms are delightful and the formal gardens have been transformed especially for outdoor weddings. On Sundays, in the summer, there is live jazz on the patio.

Gabriel's is the perfect place for special occasions, or even if you just feel like dressing up and making a special occasion for its own sake. The Douglas County News Press called Gabriel's "The Best Place to Take a Date", and Zagat's said "Highly Rated for Superb Cuisine, Ambience, and Service." The Bundys succeed in making a visit to Gabriel's "An Evening to Remember".

Executive Chef Tony Sanabria has dazzled diner's taste buds for more than ten years with signature dishes like Beef Marsala and Lobster Gorgonzola, Lamb Antonio and Scampi, jumbo shrimp sautéed in butter, white wine and Italian spices. All the mouth-watering entrees are preceded by a special appetizer, soup du jour, salad, and bread.

Matthew Bundy personally selects the over 300 wines from France, Italy, Australia, New Zealand, Spain, Chili, Argentina and the United States. Gabriel's has earned the Wine Spectator's Award of Excellence in previous years. Gabriel's Victorian home has several small, personal dining rooms in addition to the larger, beautifully appointed Milano Room. The restaurant can accommodate groups from 10 to 110 for private functions, and luncheons of 40 or more.

SMOKED SALMON PRIMAVERA
appetizer

Our Smoked Salmon Primavera appetizer is Gabriel's signature appetizer, which has alternately been served as the first course of the four-course dining experience at Gabriel's since 1985. Quite regularly it is requested even when we are offering one of our other fine appetizers such as Scampi a la Gabriel's, Sausage Marinara or Scallops Provencal. We recently had a gentleman make a reservation and request that the Smoked Salmon Primavera be served the night of his dinner, and went so far as to say he would bring in the ingredients if only Tony, the Executive Chef, would make it especially for him.

Ingredients

- 1 pound of hot smoked Alaskan king salmon
- ¼ cup diced red onions
- 1 cup (either fresh or frozen) green peas
- 1 cup (either fresh or frozen) fancy yellow whole corn
- 1 tablespoon diced pimentos

- ½-1 tablespoon Dijon mustard (per your taste)
- ½ cup heavy mayonnaise
- 6 cherry tomatoes, halved
- 6 radishes, halved
- 6 black olives, halved

Preparation

REMOVE the skin from the salmon and crumble it into a large mixing bowl. Add all remaining ingredients and fold well by hand. Salt and pepper to taste. Chill in refrigerator for 2 hours.

TO SERVE, scoop portions of chilled Smoked Salmon Primavera onto the middle of a large green lettuce leaf and garnish with a halved (each) cherry tomato, radish, and black olive.

Serves 6

Wine Suggestion: Chardonny, Benefizio Frescobaldi, 2001, Tuscany Region of Italy

CREAM OF MUSHROOM SOUP

Ingredients

1 pound fresh mushrooms (oyster, wild, shiitake, chanterelle – one type or all)	fresh chopped parsley
	½ teaspoon crushed red peppers
1 cup diced green peppers	½ teaspoon granulated garlic salt
⅓ cup diced onions	1 teaspoon dried basil
1½ cups diced carrots	1 teaspoon dried oregano
¼ cup olive oil	dash of salt
3 cups heavy whipping cream	½ teaspoon black pepper
2 cups soup stock (either vegetable or veal)	1½ tablespoons cornstarch

Preparation

SAUTÉ diced green peppers, onions and carrots in olive oil until tender. Add mushrooms and continue to sauté for one more minute.

POUR cream and soup stock into pot and bring to a boil. Take a half cup of soup base out and add cornstarch to it to create a rue. Add sautéed vegetables and bring back to a boil. Reduce heat to a simmer and add cornstarch rue to achieve desired thickness. Salt and pepper to desired taste.

SERVE immediately, as this does not need to simmer on stove. Garnish with chopped fresh parsley.

Serves 10

Wine suggestion: Pinot Grigio, Bottega Vinala, Trentino, 2002, Italy

RACK OF COLORADO LAMB
with Mint Pesto Sauce

We have chosen to use Colorado lamb to serve at Gabriel's because we love supporting our local Colorado industry and also because Colorado lamb is well known for its sweet, mild flavor and large size to the eye of the rack. We have gained the reputation of serving some of the best lamb in the Front Range.

Ingredients

Colorado rack of lamb
Dijon mustard
seasoned bread crumbs

olive oil
Mint Pesto Sauce (recipe follows)

Preparation

PREHEAT oven to 350 degrees, and heat olive oil in large non-stick skillet. Leave a generous amount of fat on rack, and rub Dijon mustard over entire rack. Lightly dust with seasoned bread crumbs. Sear prepared rack of lamb in hot olive oil to a golden brown (approximately 1 to 2 minutes for each side, depending upon size of rack). Roast in oven for 6 to 8 minutes to achieve a rare temperature to the rack (depending upon the size of the eye of the rack of lamb). Remove lamb from oven and allow it to sit for ten minutes.

For the Mint Pesto Sauce

2 *cloves of garlic*
4 *ounces fresh mint*
2 *tablespoons pine nuts*

2 *tablespoons of fresh Parmesan cheese*
½ *cup olive oil*

BLEND first four ingredients into a paste. This will take about one minute in either a blender or food processor. Do not over-blend. Then, very slowly add the olive oil, while continuing to blend. This will take about 30 seconds. Salt and pepper to taste.

TO SERVE, place Colorado Rack of Lamb on a platter, either still as a rack or cut into individual lamb cutlets and pour the Mint Pesto Sauce over the lamb.

Suggested Accompaniments Include:
Grilled asparagus that has been marinated in olive oil, steak seasoning, and salt.
Baby red potatoes, boiled to fork-tender and topped with butter, garlic, roasted red peppers, salt and pepper.

Serves 4–6

Wine Selection: Rosso di Montalcino, Castello Banfi, 2000, Tuscany Region of Italy

William F. "Buffalo Bill" Cody. (1910)

Brasserie Ten Ten

1011 Walnut
Boulder, CO 80302
303-998-1010
www.brasserietenten.com

Monday – Friday
11:00 am – 11:00
Saturday
5 pm – 11 pm
Closed Sundays

Brasserie Ten Ten
Anthony Hessel, Executive Chef

Brasserie Ten Ten brings a sharp, crisp French brasserie along Walnut Street in Boulder. The light and airy restaurant is surrounded by floor to ceiling windows, a hand-tiled marble mosaic floor, dark walnut woodwork, and café height tables in the bar area. The front of the restaurant opens up into a small patio framed by flowerbeds and an awning, to enjoy the warmth of the sun on those wistful summer days in Boulder.

Executive Chef Anthony Hessel leads his staff in the display kitchen viewable through a red-bricked archway window in the main dining area. Chef Hessel classifies his menu as "French-inspired" with a consciousness for the Boulder diner's appetite and health priorities. His sauces are lighter and entrees feature many vegetarian dishes. Classic French dishes like Coq au Vin, Bouillabaisse, and Cassoulet are also served. Try the Carre' d'Agneau (New Zealand rack of lamb), with Bartlett pear and mint mignonette, roasted garlic potato puree, and horseradish crème. The Salade Perigourdine features grilled duck breast, beef carpaccio, bacon truffle dressed greens and goat cheese. The Pommes Frites appetizer is served in a winding metal cone stand with truffled mayonnaise. The Brasserie Ten Ten appetizers also feature an extensive selection of seafood with seasonal raw oysters, poached gulf shrimp, sashimi, and Dungeness crab.

At the end of the evening, enjoy a heavenly dessert created by Pastry Chef Shamane Simons that are masterpieces both in taste and design. One of the selections is the Terrine de Mousse au Chocolat, a decadent chocolate mousse inter-layered with a pistachio almond croquant over Cognac poached pears.

To pair with any menu item, Brasserie Ten Ten's wine list features bottles from all corners of the world with price ranges to fit any dining party.

SALAD SIMPLE

Ingredients

2 ounces butter lettuce
1 tablespoon fried capers
2 teaspoons toasted pine nuts

4 cherry tomato halves
   Caper Miso Vinaigrette
   (recipe follows)

Preparation

TOSS butter lettuce with two tablespoons of caper miso vinaigrette, place in center of plate, sprinkle with fried capers and pine nuts. Place cherry tomatoes around plate.

For the Caper Miso Vinaigrette

¼ cup white miso paste
¼ cup capers, drained and rinsed
2 tablespoons Dijon mustard
1 teaspoon parsley

¼ cup red wine vinegar
½ cup of water
¾ cup canola oil
   salt and pepper to taste

IN A food processor, add miso paste, capers, mustard, parsley, water, and red wine vinegar. Pulse until smooth. With processor running slowly, add oil until completely emulsified. Season with salt and pepper.

Serves 1

TOMATO BISQUE

Ingredients

¼ cup olive oil
1 pound yellow onion, diced
½ pound leeks, white only, diced
1 tablespoon garlic, minced
2 cans peeled plum tomatoes
½ gallon vegetable stock
2 bay leaves

2 sprigs of fresh thyme
1 pound roux
1 cup cream
salt and pepper to taste
goat cheese (½ ounce) per serving
aged balsamic vinegar (a drop) per
serving

Preparation

IN A stock pot add olive oil, heat and add onions, leeks and garlic and sauté until tender.
Add 2 cans of tomatoes, vegetable stock, bay leaves, and fresh thyme. Bring to a boil and
reduce to a simmer. Add roux, salt and pepper to taste, and finish with cream. Strain and
serve.

TOP with goat cheese and aged balsamic vinegar.

Serves 2-4

Coq Au Vin

Ingredients

1 whole chicken, cut into 4 pieces	2 tablespoons olive oil
2 cups red wine	¼ pound pearl onions
1 cup beef stock	¼ pound mushrooms, sliced
2 tablespoons shallots, chopped	¼ pound smoked bacon
salt and pepper to taste	1 tablespoon butter
3 sprigs fresh rosemary	2 tablespoons goat cheese

Preparation

MIX half red wine and half beef stock in a bowl. Add shallots, pepper, and two sprigs of rosemary, place chicken in marinade overnight. In a sauté pan, add one tablespoon of olive oil and caramelize pearl onions. Add chicken and brown evenly.

ADD mushrooms, bacon, and rosemary. Deglaze with beef stock and wine, place in oven at 350 degrees for 20 minutes, remove, and reduce liquid by half. Swirl in butter and place on plate. Top with goat cheese.

Serves 4

Panoramic view of Boulder, Colorado northwest from Court House. (1870)

Flagstaff House

1138 Flagstaff Road
Boulder, CO 80301
303-442-4640
www.flagstaffhouse.com

Dinner
Sunday through Friday
6 pm - 10 pm
Saturday
5 pm – 10 pm

Flagstaff House Restaurant

Mark Monette, Executive Chef and partner

Scott and Mark Monette, partners.

The Flagstaff House Restaurant, originally a cabin built in 1929, sits nestled on the mountainside overlooking the city of Boulder, Colorado. After acquiring the property in 1971, the Monette family greatly expanded the Flagstaff House and transformed it into a world-class dining establishment, featuring floor to ceiling glass windows that allow views of the beautiful, serene mountainsides and city below, along with glimpses of deer, an occasional bear, and other wildlife that visit Flagstaff House.

The richly crafted mahogany bar, cozy fireplace, and rare crystal collected from around the world enhance the ambience. The restaurant's Vintner's Rooms offer views of the Flagstaff House's extensive 20,000 bottle wine cellar, distinguished recipient of the Wine Spectator Grand Award.

In addition to the Wine Spectator Grand Award, the Flagstaff House Restaurant was selected in 2004 for induction into the Nation's Restaurant News Fine Dining Hall of Fame, and has received the Mobil Four Star Award, Triple AAA Four Diamond Award, and the DiRoNA Award.

The cuisine is French with Asian accents. Executive Chef and partner Mark Monette, at Flagstaff House since 1985, trained in several Michelin Three Star restaurants in France and restaurants in New York City and the Orient. Mark has prepared a special menu for the Emperor and Empress of Japan, Emperor Akihito and Empress Michiko, as well as the Prime Minister of Japan, Ryutaro Hashimoto, and his foreign ministers during his time at the Flagstaff House. In addition, the restaurant has hosted many dinners for notable culinary dignitaries such as Paul Bocuse, Angela Gaja, and Robert Mondavi.

Flagstaff House, Boulder

160

 Grand Award

BUTTERNUT SQUASH SOUP
with Winter Spices

Ingredients

1 large butternut squash	½ teaspoon nutmeg
1 onion, cut thin	1 teaspoon cumin
2 ounces ginger root, cut small	1 teaspoon paprika
1 carrot, peeled and cut small	1 teaspoon salt
1 large yam, peeled and cut small	1 teaspoon white pepper
1 bulb garlic, separated and peeled	2 bay leaves
1 stick butter	¼ cup maple syrup
water to cover	½ cup heavy whipping cream
¼ teaspoon cayenne	

Preparation

CUT butternut squash in half, length-wise, and place on buttered sheet pan, seed side down. Bake at 300 degrees for 20 minutes. Remove from oven and let cool. Take out seeds and peel, then set squash aside in bowl.

COMBINE onion, ginger root, carrot, yam, and garlic in a large pot with butter. Sauté ingredients until tender.

PUT squash in pot with the other ingredients and add water until all ingredients are covered. Simmer for 2 hours.

AS soup simmers, add cayenne, nutmeg, cumin, paprika, salt, white pepper, bay leaves, and maple syrup.

SIMMER soup for 2 hours, then remove small batches and blend in a blender and strain. Finish with heavy whipping cream. Season to taste and adjust consistency with water or your favorite liquid.

Serves 6-8

JOHN DORY
with Roasted Sweet Peppers and Bananas

Ingredients

1	pound fresh John Dory fish, cleaned
1½	teaspoon butter
	juice of 1 lemon
1	small banana, diced
½	red pepper, roasted, seeded, skinned and diced

½ yellow pepper, roasted, seeded, skinned and diced
salt
white pepper

Preparation

SEASON and sauté John Dory, remove from pan. Melt butter until it stops bubbling, add lemon juice, and then add bananas, peppers, salt, and pepper to taste. Spoon mixture on to plate, place the John Dory on top, and serve.

Serves 2

Wine suggestion: This John Dory dish would pair well with a New Zealand Sauvignon Blanc.

CRISPY NOODLE-WRAPPED PORK TENDERLOIN
with Orange-Pumpkin Sauce

Ingredients

2 pork tenderloins, peeled and divided into 6-ounce portions
1 teaspoon olive oil
2 garlic cloves, chopped
2 sprigs of sage, chopped
1 package phyllo dough, shredded to resemble noodles

salt and pepper to taste
1 tablespoon oil
1 teaspoon butter
Orange Pumpkin Sauce (recipe follows)

Preparation

IN A medium sized bowl, add olive oil, garlic, sage, and the two pork tenderloins and marinate while preparing the rest of the ingredients.

SPREAD out the shredded phyllo dough and wrap it around the pork.

IN A non-stick pan over medium heat, add a tablespoon of oil, butter, and the pork. Sear pork on all sides until golden brown. Then cook pork in oven at medium high temperature for 15 minutes, checking doneness after 9 minutes. Prepare the sauce. When pork is done, cut it into several thick slices. Place 3 slices on a serving plate and serve with sauce dribbled over the top.

For the Orange Pumpkin Sauce

¼ pie pumpkin, roasted and diced
5 shallots, sliced
1 cinnamon stick
1 clove
1 star anis
5 black peppercorns
2 bay leaves
1 teaspoon thyme

1 ounce ginger
  orange zest
1 cup white wine
1 cup orange juice
2 cups veal stock
2 tablespoons maple syrup
1 tablespoon butter

Preparation

SWEAT shallots in butter until clear. Add cinnamon stick, clove, star anis, peppercorns, bay leaves, thyme, ginger, orange zest and mix thoroughly. Then add diced pumpkin and white wine, reduce to a glaze. Add orange juice and reduce. Add veal stock and maple syrup and reduce by a third. Strain, season, and stir in butter. Pour sauce sparingly over pork slices when ready to serve.

Serves 4-6

The pork tenderloin will pair well with a Pinot Noir.

BUFFALO WELLINGTON

Ingredients

16 ounces buffalo filet mignon
2 slices foie gras
   salt and pepper to taste

Brioche (recipe follows)
1 egg

Preparation

PREHEAT oven to 425 degrees. Sear whole buffalo loin in a hot pan on all sides until it is brown (approximately five minutes total) and set aside. Heat a non-stick pan until very hot. Season desired amount of the foie gras with salt and white pepper. Place the foie gras in the hot pan and sear until the edges become dark (about 45 seconds). Turn over foie gras and cook until center of foie gras feels soft in the middle (about 45 seconds). Remove from pan and pat dry with paper towel. Cool foie gras until firm.
Slice cooked buffalo lengthwise down the center to butterfly, taking care not to cut the loin completely through. Place the cooked foie gras down the center of the buffalo. Fold the buffalo so the foie gras is in the middle. Place buffalo on the brioche and wrap brioche around the buffalo completely.

THEN crack one egg into a bowl and whisk. Gently brush egg wash over the brioche wrapped buffalo. Place on baking sheet and place in preheated oven.

BAKE buffalo in preheated oven for 10 - 12 minutes, or until the dough is golden brown (or approximately medium rare). Use a meat thermometer if an exact temperature is desired (rare - 125°, medium rare - 130°, medium - 135°, medium well - 140°). Then let the meat rest for 5 - 7 minutes. Slice the buffalo down the center and serve cut side up.

For the Brioche

1½ cups high gluten flour
1 teaspoon salt
1 teaspoon sugar

2 teaspoons cake yeast
5 eggs
3 sticks soft butter

PUT all ingredients, except for butter, in mixing bowl. Using hook blade, mix well on a speed of 3 until it does not stick. Reduce mixer speed to 2 and add softened (room temperature) butter very slowly. Do not scrape sides of bowl. Once butter is completely incorporated, put mixture in refrigerator for at least 10 minutes until chilled. Then roll out the brioche so it is the same thickness as a piecrust. Use as directed in main recipe.

Serves 2

Recommended Wine: A full-bodied Cabernet Sauvignon, Syrah, or Zinfandel would pair well with this dish.

GOLDEN EGG SURPRISE

This cocoa sorbet is a signature dessert dish at Flagstaff House.

Ingredients

8 ounces sugar
4 ounces cocoa powder
   dash salt
3 cups water

1 ounce dark rum
6 edible gold foil sheet
36 fresh, ripe raspberries

Preparation

WARM sugar, cocoa powder, salt, and rum in the water, then chill for 10 minutes. Place ingredients in an ice cream freezer and spin until mixture is smooth and thickened. Group 6 raspberries on a small dessert plate. Scoop out a heaping tablespoon of the semi-frozen mixture and carefully place on top of the raspberries. Very carefully place an edible golden leaf over the top of the semi-frozen mixture and raspberries, and the gold leaf will form an egg-shape. Serve immediately and enjoy!

NOTE: Edible gold foil sheets are available at various specialty food stores or can be found online at www.shopflagstaffhouse.com.

Serves 6

View of Boulder from Flagstaff Mountain.

Vintner's room.

Flagstaff House, Boulder

165

Flagstaff House in 1950.

Greenbriar Inn

The Greenbriar Inn

Est. 1967

8735 N. Foothills Hwy.
Boulder, Colorado 80302
303-440-7979
www.greenbriarinn.com

Tuesday through Sunday
5:30 pm - 9:00 pm
Sunday Champagne Brunch
11:00 am - 2:00 pm

The Greenbriar Inn

The Greenbriar Inn has a 35-year tradition of exceptional American cuisine, fine wine and elegant service. Several long-standing awards, such as the Mobile Three Star Award and the Wine Spectator Best of Award of Excellence, have recognized this tradition.

The inn was originally built at the mouth of Left Hand Canyon in 1873 as a home, general store and post office for the town of Altona. Altona had been established as a supply and transportation center for the miners of Jamestown and Ward. With the decline of mining, the post office was closed in 1916, and the general store became a gas station in the early 1920's. It remained as such until is was purchased in 1967 and converted into the present Greenbriar Inn.

Located on 26 acres, the inn has two garden patios that offer gorgeous views of the foothills. In the spring, the lilac and hyacinth draw a variety of butterflies to the area. Inside, the building boasts two floors of elegant dining rooms with stone fireplaces, glass and porcelain chandeliers and warm wood wainscoting.

The elegant menu has something for everyone, from Colorado Lamb T-bones to Beef Wellington, to Rocky Mountain Trout and Alaskan Halibut, as well as some sumptuous vegetarian dishes. For the more adventurous, try the Spring Suckling Pig served three ways or the New England Partridge, pan-roasted and stuffed with pinenuts, sage, and brie. With their own in-house pastry chef, the inn boasts an irresistible dessert menu, so be sure to leave room for at least a taste. The Greenbriar Inn also features a lavish Champagne Sunday Brunch.

The Greenbriar wine list is a read in itself, with fifty pages packed with wines from France, Italy, Germany, Australia, New Zealand, South Africa, Spain, Argentina, Chile, and well as a very comprehensive list of American wines. An extensive dessert wine section includes 21 different ports.

Best of Award of Excellence

Greenbriar Inn, Boulder

SEARED SCALLOPS BEAUFROT
Foie Gras, Baby Artichokes, Black Truffles, Sauterne Gelée
appetizer

Ingredients

4 *jumbo scallops, cleaned*
  sea salt and fresh cracked pepper to
  taste
1 *tablespoon cooking oil*
4 *tablespoons butter*
1 *tablespoon lavender honey*
1 *ounce fresh thyme*

4 *small artichokes, steamed (recipe*
  follows)
4 *1-ounce pieces foie gras (recipe*
  follows)
  Black Truffle Vinaigrette (recipe
  follows)
  Sauterne Gelée (recipe follows)

PREHEAT non-stick sauté pan to medium high heat (the pan must be hot). Season scallops with sea salt and fresh cracked pepper. Add cooking oil to the hot sauté pan (let oil get hot). Place scallops in pan and sear on both sides. Put four tablespoons butter in the pan with the scallops. Add lavender honey and thyme and baste scallops. Reserve scallops, keep warm, and save the pan for the artichokes.

TO SERVE, warm all ingredients thoroughly, except for the sauterne gelée and truffle vinaigrette. Place artichoke on plate first, top with seared scallop, then with foie gras. Garnish with truffle vinaigrette, diced sauterne gelée, and thyme leaves.

For the Artichoke Hearts

4 *small artichokes*
4 *cups water*
1 *lemon*
1 *bay leaf*
6 *peppercorns*

4 *tablespoons salt*
1 *clove*
1 *teaspoon allspice*
4 *garlic cloves*
1 *shallot*

PREPARE court bouillon by combining water, lemon, bay leaf, peppercorns, salt, clove, allspice, garlic, and shallot. Steam artichokes in court bouillon until fork tender. Clean and reserve artichoke hearts. Place artichoke hearts in the pan where the scallops were cooked and rewarm artichoke hearts in the scallop pan just prior to serving.

For the Foie Gras

4 *1-ounce pieces of duck liver*
  sea salt
  fresh cracked pepper

SEARED SCALLOPS BEAUFROT
CONTINUED

PREHEAT non-stick sauté pan on high heat. Score the four pieces of foie gras in crosshatch pattern on the top and bottom of the liver. Season with sea salt and fresh cracked pepper. Place the liver in a very hot pan with no oil. Sear on each side until golden brown. Reserve the foie gras on the same warming plate for later.

For the Black Truffles

1 ounce black truffle shavings
1 ounce favorite sauterne
1 teaspoon truffle oil
2 tablespoons olive oil

1 tablespoon chopped chives
sea salt to taste
fresh cracked pepper to taste

PLACE all ingredients in a mixing bowl and blend. Reserve for later.

For the Sauterne Gelée

1 cup favorite sauterne
1 gelatin leaf
sea salt to taste

HEAT and reduce sauterne by half. Bloom gelatin leaf in water that is at room temperature. Incorporate gelatin leaf into the hot sauterne liquid. Season with salt. Place in a small container and chill in refrigerator. Dice sauterne gelée into small dice, once liquid has set in refrigerator.

Serves 4

WILD MUSHROOM VELOUTÉ
Lobster Custard, Coral Cream, Lemon Confit

This makes an impressive presentation. The Wild Mushroom Soup is served tableside in a soup tureen. The Lobster Custard, topped with Coral Cream and Lemon Confit, is presented in coffee cups – a chance to show off your most elegant tableware.

Ingredients

1 quart button mushrooms
1 quart portobello mushrooms, peeled,
*   gills removed*
½ quart French horn mushrooms
½ pound butter
½ yellow onion
1 shallot
3 cloves garlic
1 leek
1 celery heart

4 thyme sprigs
1 bay leaf
1 cup white wine
1 quart vegetable stock
*   salt and fresh pepper to taste*
*   Coral Whipped Cream (recipe follows)*
*   Lobster Custard (recipe follows)*
*   Lemon Confit (recipe follows)*
*   chopped chives for garnish*

Preparation

MELT butter in a large soup pot, add cleaned mushrooms. Add yellow onion, shallot, garlic, leek, celery heart, thyme, and bay leaf, then sweat all ingredients until they are soft. Deglaze with white wine and reduce by half. Add vegetable stock, bring liquid to a simmer, salt and pepper to taste. Puree soup really fine, then strain through a chinois. Reserve soup, keeping warm, until ready to serve it tableside in a soup terrine.

PREPARE coral whipped cream, lobster custard and lemon confit. When ready to serve, spoon coral whipped cream on top of lobster custard in the coffee cups. Add lemon confit garnish over coral whipped cream, and sprinkle with chopped chives. Bring coffee cups and soup tureen with wild mushroom soup to the table. To serve, pour soup gently over the custard, whipped cream, and lemon confit at the table.

For the Lobster Custard

6 egg yolks
1 cup lobster stock

4 ounces chopped lobster meat
*   salt and white pepper to taste*

SET up steamer on stovetop. Mix the egg yolks, lobster stock, and lobster meat together in a mixing bowl, until all ingredients are incorporated. Salt and pepper to taste. Spoon the lobster custard mixture into the coffee cups, using approximately ¼ cup of custard for each coffee cup. When custard is in place, cover the cups with plastic wrap. Steam custard in the steamer until custard is set. Reserve cups, keeping warm, with plastic wrap on top until needed.

WILD MUSHROOM VELOUTÉ
CONTINUED

For the Coral Cream

½ cup heavy whipping cream
2 ounces lobster roe
2 tablespoons chopped chives

juice of one lemon
salt and white pepper

WHIP cream into stiff peaks. Fold chopped lobster roe and chopped chives gently into whipped cream. Season with lemon juice, salt, and pepper and gently fold into cream. Reserve cream in refrigerator.

For the Lemon Confit

2 lemons, sliced in wheels
1 cup olive oil
  salt and white pepper

GENTLY poach the lemon wheels in olive oil for 20 minutes on low heat, salt and pepper to taste. Cool lemons in oil and reserve. Chop lemon wheels finely.

Serves 6–8

GRILLED VENISON MEDALLION
with Toasted Barley Risotto, Red Currant Conserve, Roasted Golden Beets, Sage Butter

Ingredients

4 5-ounce venison medallions
6 juniper berries, crushed
4 garlic cloves, crushed
12 black peppercorns
1 tablespoon fresh sage, chopped
¼ cup olive oil
  kosher salt to taste

fresh pepper to taste
Toasted Barley Risotto (recipe follows)
Roasted Golden Beets (recipe follows)
Venison Jus (recipe follows)
Red Currant Conserve (recipe follows)
Sage Leaves (recipe follows)
Sage Butter (recipe follows)

Preparation

THE day before, mix juniper berries, garlic cloves, peppercorns, chopped sage, and olive oil together in a mixing bowl to create a marinade. Rub venison medallions with marinade and let them rest overnight, refrigerated.

THE day of the meal, prepare the barley risotto, beets, red currant conserve, fried sage leaves, sage butter, and venison jus, using directions below.

TO GRILL the medallions, clean off marinade and re-season with kosher salt and fresh cracked black pepper. Grill the meat to rare and let it rest five to ten minutes.

TO SERVE, put toasted barley on plate first, then place sliced, roasted golden beets at the top of the plate. Slice venison and place at the bottom of the plate. Add the venison jus to the plate and garnish with red currant conserve, fried sage leaves, and one wheel of sage butter.

For the Toasted Barley Risotto

6 cups vegetable stock
2 cups toasted barley
1 ounce olive oil
¼ onion, minced
1 clove garlic, chopped
½ cup white wine

1 tablespoon unsalted butter
½ cup grated Manchego cheese
1 tablespoon fresh, chopped parsley
kosher salt to taste
ground white pepper to taste

WARM vegetable stock in a saucepot. Toast barley in the oven until it is golden brown. In a second saucepot, add oil, onion, and garlic. Sweat lightly. Add barley to onions and garlic, cook barley for two minutes. Deglaze the pot with white wine, stirring occasionally. Continue to add the warm stock to the barley, stirring in several stages until all the stock is incorporated into the barley. Finish the barley with butter, Manchego cheese, and chopped parsley. Season accordingly.

For the Roasted Golden Beets

2 large golden beets
1 tablespoon olive oil
salt and pepper to taste

RUB beets with oil. Salt and pepper the beets, keeping skin intact. Roast beets at 300 degrees for 2½ - 3 hours, until fork tender. Peel the beet skins off, fan sliced beets and re-roast just prior to assembling plate.

For the Venison Jus

chopped mirepoix
1 bunch sage
5 peppercorns
2 cups red wine

4 cups veal stock
roasted venison bone
kosher salt to taste

CARAMELIZE the mirepoix in a saucepot, add sage and peppercorns to the pot, then deglaze with red wine, reducing by half. Add the veal stock and venison bone to the pot and simmer for three hours. Strain and reduce to a sauce consistency. Season as needed.

GRILLED VENISON MEDALLION
CONTINUED

For the Red Currant Conserve

  1 tablespoon red wine vinegar
    zest of one orange
  1 tablespoon honey
  1 tablespoon brown sugar
  ½ cup port wine

  ¼ cup orange juice
  ¼ cup red currants
    kosher salt to taste
    fresh pepper to taste

COMBINE the red wine vinegar, orange zest, honey, and brown sugar in a saucepot and reduce it until the liquid starts to caramelize. Deglaze saucepot with the port wine and reduce to a syrup-like consistency. Then deglaze the saucepot with the orange juice and reduce. Stop cooking and fold in the red currants, letting the currants steep in the saucepot until the conserve is room temperature. Season to taste.

For Fried Sage Leaves

  12 sage leaves
   1 cup frying oil

HEAT oil to 250 degrees. Remove stems from the sage leaves and drop them into the fryer, one at a time. The leaves will crackle, and once they no longer crackle, remove them from the oil, and place on an absorbent towel.

For the Sage Butter

  ⅛ pound of butter
  6 leaves of sage

  1 teaspoon kosher salt
  1 teaspoon fresh cracked pepper

SOFTEN butter until it is room temperature. Mix all ingredients together, roll into a log shape in waxed paper. Let the butter set in the refrigerator. Once the butter is cool and can maintain its shape, cut it into wheels.

Serves 4

CANDIED GINGER WALNUT CAKE
with Caramelized Pears

Ingredients

1 cup walnut pieces
1 cup sugar
1 cup butter, soft
2 tablespoons dark corn syrup
1 tablespoon canola oil
1½ cups all-purpose flour
3 tablespoons cornstarch
1 teaspoon baking powder

3 tablespoons candied ginger, minced
4 eggs
   Pear William Cinnamon Semifreddo
   (recipe follows)
   Ginger Crème Anglaise (recipe follows)
   Poached Pears (recipe follows)
   Pear Chips (recipe follows)
   candied walnut halves (optional)

Preparation

PREHEAT oven to 325 degrees. Chop walnuts and sugar in food processor until smooth. Transfer to a bowl, then add butter, corn syrup, and oil. Cream until smooth. Add flour, cornstarch, baking powder, ginger, and eggs. Cream until smooth. Fill 12 individual miniature bundt cake pans ⅔ full, bake at 325 degrees about 30-40 minutes or until cake bounces back when touched lightly. Set aside until needed.

TO SERVE, unmold semifreddo, slice in half. Place the two half moons slightly apart on the middle of the plate. Top with individual walnut cake, spoon warm pears over the top, allowing a few to fall into spaces created between the semifreddo half moons. Spoon ginger anglaise on to the plate, next to the pears and semifreddo, drizzling some on to the pears. Garnish with pear chips and candied walnut halves.

For the Pear William Cinnamon Semifreddo

6 egg yolks
½ cup sugar
⅓ cup Williams Pear liquor

2 tablespoons vanilla
¼ teaspoon cinnamon
2 cups heavy cream

BEAT yolks until fluffy. Continue to beat while adding sugar, liquor, vanilla, and cinnamon, beating until fluffy. Cook over bain-marie, whisking constantly until thick and alcohol cooks off. Remove from heat and whisk until cool. Beat heavy cream until it forms soft peaks. Whisk ¼ of cream into custard mix and fold in remaining cream gently. Pipe into desired mold shapes (3" round molds) about ½ inch thick and freeze.

CANDIED GINGER WALNUT CAKE
CONTINUED

For the Ginger Crème Anglaise

3 egg yolks
5 tablespoons sugar
1 cup Half & Half

¼ vanilla bean or ¾ teaspoon vanilla extract
½ teaspoon candied ginger, minced

COMBINE yolks and sugar, whisk until light and fluffy. Scald Half & Half with the vanilla bean. While whisking, gradually pour the Half & Half into the yolk mixture and add ginger. Place mixture over simmering water, heat slowly, stirring constantly until it's thick enough to coat the back of a spoon. Do not heat over 190 degrees, or the mixture will curdle. Add vanilla extract (if you didn't use the vanilla bean earlier) and strain through a fine mesh strainer or chinois.

For the Poached Pears

2 ounces butter
5 ounces sugar
4 medium Bosc pears

PEEL and slice pears into wedges so that there are at least 12 wedges per pear. Heat butter with sugar until bubbly and light brown. Add pear slices and cook, stirring constantly until soft.

For the Pear Chips

1 pear
1 cup water

1 cup granulated sugar
2-4 drops lemon juice

TO MAKE simple syrup, mix sugar and water, add a few drops of lemon juice, and bring to a boil for one minute. Slice the pear thinly, and drop the slices briefly into the simmering simple syrup. Place pears on non-stick silicone mat, on baking pan, and bake between 2-3 hours at 200 degrees, until dry and crisp.

Serves 12

Red Lion

38470 Boulder Canyon
Boulder, CO 80302
303-442-9368
www.redlionrestaurant.com

Monday-Sunday
5:00 pm to close

The Red Lion Restaurant

Christoph and Heidi Mueller, Owners

Located just four beautiful miles outside of Boulder, up the winding Boulder Canyon Drive, is a lovely setting in the pine-covered hills. The original building comprising the heart of the Red Lion was built in 1870, and has been expanded and remodeled several times. It now consists of eight different rooms on two floors of the house, along with outside seating on the patio overlooking a bubbling creek. The bar sports a pot-bellied stove and stone walls. The original dining room creates the feeling of dining in the Alps with Austrian murals, game antlers and a fireplace.

In July 2003, the owners, Christoph and Heidi Mueller celebrated forty years of operating the Red Lion. Their German background can be seen in some of the specialty dishes on the menu, along with the great variety of game meats that are served: elk, buffalo, wild boar, pheasant, quail, and a variety of game sausages. You can also try a variety of the game with the appetizer sampler platters to test the waters before you dive in to the main course.

For that main course, you might want to try the Hickory Smoked "New Zealand" Venison Rack, basted with Canadian whiskey, and served over sweet potato mash with huckleberry sauce, grapes, mushrooms, and bacon. Or try the farm Raised Pheasant Breast filled with forest mushrooms, sun dried cherries and topped with a brandy peppercorn sauce. If fish is your desire, enjoy the Rocky Mountain Trout served over roasted potatoes with lump crab and lemon beurre blanc.

This is the place to bring your out-of-town guests, after a day of hiking in the canyon or enjoying Boulder Creek Falls. Your attire can be casual to formal, just bring your adventurous appetite.

Chris and Heidi

GERMAN BEEF SAUERBRATEN

This is a great dish for a family gathering. Serve with German spatzle and pickled red cabbage.

Ingredients

3½ pounds beef eye of round, denuded
2 ounces raisins, softened in water
4 pieces gingerbread, crumbled
1 tablespoon red currant jelly

1 cup heavy cream
½ cup red wine
salt and pepper to taste
Marinade (recipe follows)

Preparation

TWO to three days before serving, make marinade and marinate beef eye of round in refrigerator.

THE day you plan to serve the sauerbraten, take the beef pieces out of the marinade and pat dry with a kitchen towel. Preheat oven to 350 degrees. Season the meat and brown on all sides in a roasting pan.

STRAIN roasting vegetables out of the marinade and reserve marinade.
Add vegetables to the roasting pan and roast on all sides, add marinade and cook in oven for 2-3 hours, or until fork tender.

REMOVE from oven and cool for 30 minutes. Take meat out of the sauce and keep warm. Strain sauce into a saucepan and thicken with raisins, gingerbread, and red currant jelly. Simmer for 10-15 minutes.

IN A blender, mix sauce until smooth, strain, add heavy cream and red wine, and season to taste. Cut beef into half-inch slices and arrange on a platter, pour sauce over the meat and serve.

GERMAN BEEF SAUERBRATEN
CONTINUED

For the Marinade

2½ cups water
1½ cups red wine vinegar
1 teaspoon salt
10 peppercorns, crushed
10 juniper berries, crushed
5 cloves
½ teaspoon mustard seed

3 onions, peeled and sliced
1 carrot, cleaned and sliced
2 bay leaves
1 cup red wine
  coriander to taste
  marjoram to taste
  rosemary to taste

COMBINE all ingredients.

Wine suggestion: German Blau Burgundy or any French Burgundy or Cabernet

Serves 8

GRILLED MARINATED QUAIL, BARLEY RISOTTO AND RASPBERRIES

Ingredients

- 6 quail, semi-boneless
- ½ cup raspberries
- 2 tablespoons olive oil
- 1 tablespoon raspberry vinegar
- 1 tablespoon honey
- ½ teaspoon garlic, minced
- 1 dash rosemary, chopped
- 1 dash thyme, chopped
- salt and pepper
- Barley Risotto (recipe follows)
- fresh raspberries for garnish (optional)
- fresh herbs for garnish (optional)

Preparation

COMBINE raspberries, olive oil, raspberry vinegar, honey, garlic, rosemary, and thyme. Place quail in a bowl and mix to coat. Let it marinate for two hours or overnight.

REMOVE quail from marinade and wipe off excess. Season with salt and pepper and grill on both sides for two or three minutes.

TO SERVE, scoop two tablespoons of barley risotto, place grilled quail on top, garnish with balsamic syrup, raspberry coulis, fresh raspberries and fresh herbs.

For the Barley Risotto

- ½ cup barley
- 1 tablespoon olive oil
- 2 shallots, minced
- 2 tablespoons brunoise, assorted vegetables
- ¼ cup mushrooms, sliced
- ¼ cup white wine
- 1½ cups chicken stock
- 1 tablespoon butter
- ¼ cup Asiago cheese, shredded

HEAT olive oil in a heavy pan. Add shallots and cook until translucent. Add barley, vegetable brunoise, and mushrooms. Stir to coat.

ADD white wine and reduce slightly. Add half of the chicken stock and simmer on low heat, stirring occasionally. Add the remaining half of the chicken stock and simmer until almost done, add butter and Asiago cheese.

Serves 6

Wine suggestion: Pepi Willamette Valley Oregon Pinot Grigio

CHATEAUBRIAND OF COLORADO BUFFALO

This is an exceptional dish, perfect for a special celebration, such as a birthday, wedding anniversary, or notable achievement.

Ingredients

1½ pounds buffalo, Chateaubriand cut
    Marinade (recipe follows)

Truffle Butter (recipe follows)
Cabernet Glaze (recipe follows)

Preparation

PLACE steak in a shallow baking dish, pour marinade over the meat, cover with plastic wrap, and marinate in the refrigerator for 24 hours.

TO PREPARE, heat a cast-iron skillet over medium heat. Take steak out of the marinade, pat dry with paper towels, and char on all sides to desired doneness. Let rest for five minutes.

TO SERVE, cut steak into ½ inch slices, drizzle some glaze on each plate and set steak on top. Cut butter into ½ inch slices, place one slice of truffle butter on top of each steak.

For the Marinade

½ cup orange juice
¼ cup white balsamic vinegar
¼ cup granulated sugar
¼ cup shallot, minced

1 tablespoon Thai chili sauce
½ teaspoon kosher salt
1 teaspoon black pepper, cracked

MIX all ingredients in a bowl.

For the Cabernet Glaze

1 cup Cabernet Sauvignon
½ cup balsamic vinegar
2 tablespoons granulated sugar

¼ teaspoon kosher salt
⅛ teaspoon black pepper, cracked

BRING all ingredients to a boil in a saucepan, then lower heat to a simmer until reduced to a light syrup. Remove from heat, reserve, and keep warm.

For the Truffle Butter

4 tablespoons butter, salted, softened
1 tablespoon black truffle, brunoise
1 tablespoon chives, thinly sliced

1 teaspoon black truffle oil
½ lemon, juiced
salt and pepper

MIX all ingredients in a bowl until smooth. Place the flavored butter mixture on a 10" X 15" piece of parchment paper, roll into a 1½ inch thick cylinder, and refrigerate.

Serves 4

Wine suggestion: Chateau Latour "Pauillac"

View from the patio.

Relaxing on the deck.

Rock climbers in Boulder Canyon.

The Savoy

Restaurant Francais
535 3rd Street
Berthoud, CO 80513
970-532-4095
www.berthoudcolorado.com

Tuesday – Saturday
5:30 pm - 9:30 pm
Sunday
4:00 pm - 9:00 pm

Savoy Restaurant
Jean and Chantal Martini, Owners
Jean Martini, Chef

Jean Martini and Chantal met at La Grillade in Paris, France. Chantal owned La Grillade and Jean was a regular customer. Chantal invited Jean to cook for the restaurant, and six months later they were married. The two came to the United States, settling in Los Angeles. In 1992, Jean and Chantal bought the Savoy in 1992, after they fell in love with the mountains and surrounding area of Berthoud.

The Savoy experience begins at the door. The intricately carved wooden door, to be precise. It opens into a room that is warm and friendly, the dark wood interior brightened by the stained-glass lamps, creating a romantic setting for the fabulous food to come.

The Savoy is known as a taste of France in the small town of Berthoud, not only for the food, but the extensive wine list, which features many French wines. The service is attentive, but not intrusive.

The menu features carefully created selections that reflect Jean and Chantal's innovative approach. Appetizers include Escargots poached in Burgundy with Roquefort Butter, and Frog Legs sautéed in garlic butter sauce. The menu varies with daily specials of fresh seafood and fish, and the Game of the Week (which in the past has included wild hare, kangaroo and duck.) Regular features at this time include Mallard Duck, Sweet Breads and Quail, all with soup, salad and vegetable accompaniments.

Jean began cooking when he was fourteen years old, and trained for three years in France, then worked as Yves Menes' right hand man at the Jonathan Club in Los Angeles. Chantal also has a long history of culinary excellence. Her grandmother was one of the first female chefs in France to receive the coveted Cordon Bleu award, and her family background in the business has been a great asset in Savoy's success.

It's well worth the 25-mile trip from Denver to experience the Savoy.

GRILLED SCALLOPS IN HONEY ORANGE HAZELNUT DRESSING
with *Julienne of Orange Peel in Tomato Florist*
appetizer

Ingredients

18 fresh jumbo scallops
2 tablespoons olive oil
   Honey Orange Hazelnut Dressing
   (recipe follows)

   Julienne of Orange Peel (recipe
   follows)
   Tomato Florist (recipe follows)

PREPARE dressing, orange peel, and tomato florist. Wash the scallops and dry with a paper towel. Brush each scallop with olive oil. Grill over medium heat for two minutes on each side (for a medium rare scallop).

TO SERVE, arrange three scallops at the bottom of the plate side by side. Place tomato florist at the top center. Trot a small amount of honey orange hazelnut dressing on each scallop and in the tomato florist. Garnish each scallop with a julienne of orange peel.

For the Honey Orange Hazelnut Dressing

3 ounces fresh squeezed orange juice
4 tablespoons hazelnut oil
2 tablespoons sherry wine vinegar

1 tablespoon honey
   salt and pepper to taste

MIX all ingredients in dressing bowl and set aside.

For the Julienne of Orange Peel

4 ounces water
1 teaspoon sugar

18 strings julienned orange peel

BRING water and sugar to a boil. Put orange peel in boiling mixture for one minute. Remove, strain and set aside.

GRILLED SCALLOPS IN HONEY ORANGE HAZELNUT DRESSING
CONTINUED

For the Tomato Florist

6 Roma tomatoes	60 enoki mushrooms
water for cooking	6 leaves of radicchio
ice water	6 red leafs
6½ leaves Belgium endive	6 leaves of curly endive

CUT a shallow "X" in the bottom of each tomato. Remove the stem area from the top of each tomato. Place tomatoes in boiling water for one minute. Remove and place in ice water. Peel. Cut ¼ inch off the top and remove the meat from the tomato. Cut the bottom of the tomatoes so that they will stand up on a plate. Stuff each tomato with one of each of the leaves, and ten mushrooms.

Serves 6

Wine suggestion: Vouvray Demi Sec

The Savoy's dining room.

Pan-Seared Halibut

with Fresh Beet Sauce, Asparagus, Wild Rice

Ingredients

6   5-ounce pieces of halibut filet
2   ounces clarified butter
    salt and white pepper to taste
6   edible pansies

Asparagus (recipe follows)
Wild Rice (recipe follows)
Beet Sauce (recipe follows)

Preparation

USING a non-stick pan, sear the halibut face down in clarified butter for one and a half minutes. Place in oven for 4 minutes at 375 degrees for medium rare. For medium, turn, and cook for 3 more minutes. Salt and pepper to taste. Prepare asparagus, rice, and beet sauce.

TO SERVE, steam and place asparagus in a "V" from the center of the plate up toward top. Put rice mold in center of asparagus "V". Using a two-ounce ladle, pour sauce on lower half of plate. Using a spatula, take each filet and let drain, and press with a paper towel to remove excess moisture. Place over sauce on plate. Decorate with one edible pansy at point of "V" of asparagus.

For the Asparagus

12 medium asparagus tips (3 inches in
    length)
1   quart water

    pinch of salt
1   quart of cold water and ice

PEEL asparagus. Place water in a pan with salt. Bring water to a boil, add asparagus, and boil for four minutes. While asparagus is boiling, prepare a bowl with water and ice. When asparagus is cooked, place in bowl with ice and water and set aside until needed.

For the Wild Rice

4   ounces wild rice
2   cups cold water
1   ounce each red, green and yellow bell
    pepper

½   tablespoon fresh garlic, crushed
1   ounce extra virgin olive oil
1   pinch salt
1   pinch white pepper

Pan-Seared Halibut

with Fresh Beet Sauce, Asparagus, Wild Rice

CONTINUED

WASH the rice and dry. Place rice in cold water and bring to a boil, cover loosely with foil. Place over low heat for 20-25 minutes. While the rice is cooking, prepare a brunoise of yellow, red, and green peppers. Sweat the peppers and garlic in olive oil until tender or until transparent. When rice is cooked, add brunoise, add salt and pepper to taste, mix together and put rice in two-ounce soufflé cups and cover with clear film. Press firmly into the cup to make a mold.

For the Beet Sauce

16 ounces whole fresh beets	2 ounces extra virgin olive oil
½ ounce shallots, chopped very fine	½ cup clam juice
2 bay leaves	1 tablespoon cornstarch
5 whole black peppercorns	2 tablespoons cold water

PEEL the beets, and place them in a vegetable juicer. Extract 10 ounces of beet juice. Sweat shallots, bay leaves, peppercorns, and olive oil together until transparent. Add clam juice and reduce by half. Add beet juice and bring to a boil. Remove from burner. In a cup mix cold water and cornstarch. Add cornstarch mixture to beet sauce and blend with a rubber spatula. Strain in fine chinois, then keep warm in water bath.

Serves 6

Wine suggestion: California Sauvignon Blanc or Pinot Noir

LOBSTER IN WHITE BUTTER CREAM SAUCE

Beurre blanc, or white butter cream sauce, can be used with any seafood.

Ingredients

2 1½-2 pound live large-clawed lobsters
4 stalks of celery, sliced
3 carrots, sliced
3 yellow onions, sliced

4 bay leaves
5 sprigs thyme
20 black peppercorns
   Beurre Blanc (recipe follows)

Preparation

IN TWO gallons of water, bring the vegetables and seasonings to a boil. Add lobsters and boil for 10 minutes. Remove from water. If serving cold or not serving immediately, plunge the lobsters into ice water to cool. To free meat, wrap a towel around the tail and squeeze until the shell cracks and meat can be removed. Use a mallet to crack the claws.

TO SERVE, arrange meat of one lobster on each plate and cover with sauce.

For the Beurre Blanc

6 tablespoons unsalted butter
2 bay leaves
5 black peppercorns
½ cup shallots, diced
½ cup dry white wine

1 cup heavy cream
8 tablespoons unsalted butter
2 pinches white pepper
2 pinches salt

TO CLARIFY butter, melt butter in a heavy saucepan over low heat. Remove pan from heat and let butter stand 3 minutes. Skim froth and strain butter into a bowl through a sieve lined with a double thickness of cheesecloth that's been rinsed and squeezed. There should be a milky solid residue in the bottom of pan. Pour clarified butter into a jar or crock and chill, covered. Butter keeps this way indefinitely. When clarified, butter loses about one-fourth its original volume.

IN A saucepan, over medium heat, add clarified butter, bay leaves, black peppercorns, and shallots. Sweat until the shallots are tender and transparent, but not brown. Add white wine and reduce 90 percent. Add cream and reduce by half. Whisk in butter bit by bit, stirring constantly. Add salt and pepper and whisk again. Pour sauce through a strainer.

Serves 2

Wine suggestion: Chablis or Chardonnay

BABY RACK OF LAMB IN PUFF PASTRY

Ingredients

14-16 ounces baby rack of lamb, French cut
     salt and black pepper
10 ounces mushrooms, such as
     Champignon de Paris
2 tablespoons shallots, minced
2 tablespoons clarified butter
1 tablespoon tarragon
2 pinches salt

2 pinches white pepper
1 teaspoon + 1 tablespoon heavy
     cream
     frozen puff pastry dough
     (1 sheet, 10 x 15)
3 eggs - separated, use whites for egg
     wash
2 ounces puree of goose liver

Preparation

HAVE butcher clean the rack of lamb. Salt and pepper the rack on both sides. Pan sear the rack in a hot pan for 3 minutes on each side. Remove from the pan and cool in the refrigerator for 15 minutes.

WHILE it is cooling, prepare your duxelles of mushroom. Grind the mushrooms very finely in a food processor, and sweat them in clarified butter with shallots, tarragon, salt and white pepper. Add a teaspoonful of heavy cream and cook the duxelles until dry. Cool.

REMOVE the puff pastry from the freezer and defrost at room temperature. Mix egg yolks and 1 tablespoon of heavy cream. Remove rack of lamb from the refrigerator and coat it with the duxelles of mushroom. Place the rack on the puff pastry and place two slices of goose liver on the fat side of the lamb.

FOLD the puff pastry around the rack. Pierce holes in the dough to allow the bones to protrude. Use more egg wash to "glue" the dough together, then coat the outside of the pastry with the remaining egg wash.

MAKE two little "chimneys" in the top of the dough on the fat side of the rack to prevent the dough from becoming soggy.

COOK the rack in a 400 degree oven for about 15 minutes for rare-medium rare.

Serves 4

Wine suggestion: St. -Emilian Grand Cru or good California merlot

Mango Papaya in Triangle Phyllo
with Fresh Raspberry Coulis

Ingredients

18 sheets of 16 x 6 phyllo dough
1 mango, diced very fine
1 papaya, diced very fine

3 ounces clarified butter
Raspberry Coulis (recipe follows)
mint leaf, for garnish

Preparation

BRUSH one sheet of phyllo dough with clarified butter. Place another sheet on top of that sheet and brush with butter. Place a third sheet and brush with butter. Repeat to make 6 three-layered phyllo sheets. Place all six three layered sheets side by side and place one ounce of papaya and one ounce of mango on each phyllo sheet at the corner and fold sheet over fruit to make a triangle shape. Fold over as many times as possible, creating a triangle pillow (like folding a flag). Seal with clarified butter. Fold remaining five just like above. Place triangles in a large non-stick pan and put in oven at 375 degrees for 5 minutes on each side.

TO SERVE, ladle one ounce of raspberry coulis on 9" plate. Place phyllo triangle on center of the plate with a mint leaf to garnish.

For the Raspberry Coulis

6 ounces dry champagne
6 ounces cool water

4 ounces sugar
1 pound fresh or frozen raspberries

PLACE all ingredients in a pan and bring to a boil. Cook over low heat for 20 minutes. Remove from heat and put in a food processor on high for thirty seconds. Remove from food processor and pour through a chinois, then strain a second time through a fine chinois. Let cool to room temperature

Serves 6

Wine suggestion: Champagne or Navarro Late Harvest or Sauternes

Trolley number 26 passes through the busy intersection of College Avenue and Mountain Avenue in Fort Collins. (1942).

Braddy's
Downtown
Restaurant

160 W. Oak Street
Fort Collins, CO 80524
970-498-0873
www.braddys.com

Monday - Thursday
4 pm – 10 pm
Friday and Saturday
4 pm – 11 pm
Closed Sundays

Braddy's Downtown Restaurant

Don Braddy, Co-owner and Chef
Grayson Braddy, Co-owner

Don Braddy, co-owner and chef, moved to Fort Collins at age 7, in 1968. His love of the local environment has kept him tied to the area ever since. Having cooked his way through college and part way through graduate school at Colorado State, Don realized that the restaurant business was in his soul.

After serving tenures at several fine Fort Collins restaurants, Don and Grayson Braddy opened up their restaurant in June 2001. A former appliance store, the building offered beautiful floor to ceiling windows that look out across the street to the old courthouse with its hanging tree. Another unusual oddity about the view is the set of still-used railroad tracks that run right down the center of the street. It is an interesting sight to see cars driving on both sides of the oncoming train in the middle of town.

The décor is a nice balance of nature with a chic style of fabrics, art, and contemporary furniture. Don's personal touch of putting aspen trees along both sides of the entryway, brings a little of the outdoors that he so loves into his restaurant. The newly built stone fireplace adds special warmth to the main dining room.

Don's style of cuisine is a song of praise for the use of fresh local ingredients as well as the special procurement of fresh ingredients from other parts of the world. The menu attests to the fact that most of the seafood is purchased on the docks of Honolulu, and is shipped overnight to the restaurant, making it just about as fresh as you can get it in Hawaii.

Don Braddy at the bar.

The lover of comfort food will feel right at home with the Roasted Half Free-range Chicken or the Bacon Wrapped Filet Mignon with Cabernet Sauvignon Jus. The more adventurous diner will have much to choose from, such as Texas Black Antelope with Sautéed Mushrooms, Sage, Roasted Garlic and Polenta or Mahi-Mahi with Pomegranate Chili Sauce, Sesame Basmati Rice, and Jicama & Pepper Sauté.

GRILLED SALMON
with Avocado/Pineapple-Ginger Reduction

Experimenting for a wine dinner, the Sauvignon Blanc we were working with demanded grapefruit. Well, the grapefruit wouldn't grill, but avocado and grapefruit go so well together.... but the recipe actually evolved into this....

Ingredients

½ ripe extra sweet pineapple
2 tablespoons fresh ginger, sliced
2 tablespoons rice vinegar
   dash of sea salt

1 avocado
1 pound wild salmon fillet, cut into 4 small fillets

Preparation

REMOVE the skin and core from the pineapple and slice thinly. Place with ginger in 8-quart saucepan, cover with water, and boil until tender. Puree using a hand or immersion blender, as you will want the water and its flavor. Strain through a fine sieve.

HEAT a grill or barbecue.

PLACE pureed pineapple into a sauté or sauce pan, add rice vinegar, and reduce until thick enough to coat a spoon (or desired consistency). Season with a touch of sea salt.

WHILE the sauce is reducing, season the salmon and place it on the grill. Slice the avocado half into 8 slices, coat liberally with canola oil spray, season with salt and pepper, and place, sprayed side down, on grill. The avocado will only take a minute or two or three to grill, and you will need a thin, straight spatula to remove it.

TURN the salmon when half done (maybe 3 minutes) and finish to desired temperature.

FAN avocado slices onto center of plate. Spoon sauce around avocado, and place salmon partially covering the avocado (or suitably pleasing arrangement).

Serves 4

Enjoy with friends and a nice Pinot Grigio.

COLORADO LAMB LOIN
with Minted Butternut Couscous

The best lamb in the world comes from Colorado, and we keep trying to find new ways to work with the classic mint-lamb pairing. This is a great autumn dish, as the butternut squash comes in at the end of our farmer's market season.

Ingredients

- 1 pound boneless Colorado lamb loin, fat cap on
- 1 butternut squash
- 1 ounce fresh mint, picked and washed
  olive oil for cooking
- 2 teaspoons garlic, minced
- 4 tablespoons sweet onion, minced

- 8 ounces couscous
- 1 Anaheim pepper, julienned
- 1 red bell pepper, julienned
- ½ large jicama, julienned
- 2 tablespoons unsalted butter, softened
  salt and pepper to taste

Preparation

TAKE half of the butternut squash, peel, roast or boil, then puree and strain. Take the other half and dice it to ⅜ inches and roast.

SCORE the fat cap of the lamb, liberally season both sides with salt and pepper. Render the fat by placing lamb fat side down in sauté pan over medium heat. When fat is crisp and half rendered, transfer the lamb to a sheet pan and place in preheated 300 degree oven. Roast to desired doneness, about 15 minutes for medium rare.

WHILE the lamb is cooking, place a liberal amount of good olive oil in a sauté pan, and, over medium high heat, add the garlic and onion. Sauté until just browning, then add the couscous and stir to coat the pasta. Add water and a dash of salt (and a touch of veal stock, if you have some) until just covering the pasta, and bring heat to high. When the pasta boils, reduce heat to maintain a strong, but not rolling boil. Add water as needed. After about 10 or 12 minutes, the pasta should be close to al dente, so watch the water level, as you will want a risotto-like consistency when done. Add butternut squash, puree to al dente pasta without too much water in it. Add butter and mint just before service.

AS COUSCOUS is being finished, heat a small sauté pan for the vegetables. When hot, add olive oil, peppers, and jicama. Cook for 2-3 minutes, then add diced butternut squash. Finish with a touch of butter (taking the sauté pan from the heat) and season with salt and pepper.

PLACE couscous on middle of plates, and top with vegetables. Remove lamb from oven and let rest for 5 minutes or so. Slice lamb thinly, and fan onto plate and serve.

Extra Touch:

REDUCE 1 cup red wine with 1 cup red wine vinegar and ¼ cup sugar. Reduce until slightly thick in pan (as it cools it will get thicker, and it must be easily spoonable). Let cool in refrigerator. When cool, puree more mint into the reduction, then strain the leaves out, leaving the mint infused into the syrup. Spoon onto lamb just before service.

Serves 4

We enjoy this dish with a spicy California Zinfandel.

Braddy's interior

BANANA SPLAT
(not a banana split)

During the extremely hot summer of '02 we decided we needed to do something a little more with ice cream – something to push it over the top. Given our fondness for reconstructing classics, we ended up with something that clearly was not a banana split....

Ingredients

1 banana, halved lengthwise
¼ ripe papaya, chopped to ¼ inch
4 strawberries, chopped to ¼ inch
   50/50 sugar to dark chili powder, mixed

2 medium scoops vanilla ice cream
3 tablespoons whipped cream
1 tablespoon Cilantro Syrup
   (recipe follows)

Preparation

SPRINKLE sugar/chili mix somewhat liberally over insides of halved banana evenly. With a blowtorch, carefully caramelize the sugar, taking care not to burn the chili. Mix the fruit together. Lay the halved banana in a bowl or plate so that it forms a butterfly pattern. Place chopped fruit on either side of banana. Add scoops of ice cream on top of banana.
Top with whipped cream. Garnish liberally with cilantro syrup.

For the Cilantro Syrup

1½ tablespoons water
1½ tablespoons sugar
cilantro to taste

MAKE a simple syrup with approximately 1:1 ratio of water to sugar. Let cool, then blend in cilantro with a hand blender. Strain out the cilantro with a fine sieve, and then serve. Do not do more than one day in advance.

Makes one splat, serves 1-2

I like this one best with a fine Cognac, but a dash of Chateau d'Yquem will do in a pinch.

Jay's Bistro

135 W. Oak Street
Fort Collins, CO 80524
970-482-1876

Monday - Friday
11:00 am – 10:00 pm
Saturday
5:00 pm – 10:00 pm
Sunday
5:00 pm – 8:00 pm

Jacob, Jacki, and Jay.

Jay's Bistro
Jay and Jacki Witlen, Owners
Jay Witlen, Chef

Locally known as the swankiest restaurant in Fort Collins, Jay's Bistro is a splendid example of superb interior design. The contemporary design is unique and graceful, with one room flowing into another. The large L-shaped wood bar complements the warm colors and contemporary lighting of the interior. Guests who stop at the bar for a libation preceding their dinner can get a preview of the evening soups. The soup kettles are built into one end of the bar, and emit tantalizing fragrances.

Jay and Jacki Witlen have been restaurateurs in Fort Collins since 1981. Jay originally came to Colorado with high aspirations to become a ski bum. But this self-proclaimed food junkie and avid culinary reader loved to cook. Since everyone seemed to like his cooking, he just kept at it, culminating in this, his latest accomplishment.

The building at 135 West Oak Street had originally been the location of the Poudre Valley Creamery. After that, it served a long tenure as the Brown's Shoe Fit Building, a company that sold shoes until the late 1970's. It then transferred to several operators of retail businesses until Jay and Jacki purchased the building in 2000 and completely renovated it. They envisioned four distinct dining spaces, a large cocktail lounge/bar area and a patio. The cocktail lounge hosts live jazz Thursday through Saturday evenings featuring some of the finest jazz musicians in Northern Colorado.

American cuisine dominates the menu along with delicious offerings from the oyster bar. The seafood entrees have a note that all of the seafood is line caught. The duck entrée is a trio of Confit of Duck Leg, Grilled Muscovy Duck Breast and Duck Eggroll with Asian Five Spice Hoisin Sauce over Wilted Spinach. Another creative entrée is the Mixed Grill Trilogy, composed of a Petit Filet Mignon, Ostrich on Huckleberry Pinot Sauce and Elk Medallion on Cabernet Reduction.

Y Award of Excellence

CORIANDER CRUSTED TUNA
On Ponzu Soy Sauce

Ingredients

4 6-ounce tuna steaks
3 tablespoons coriander
3 tablespoons cumin
3 tablespoons sesame seeds

oil for searing
Whipped Potatoes (recipe follows)
Ponzu Sauce (recipe follows)

Preparation

MIX coriander, cumin, and sesame seeds to make crust. Encrust tuna and pan sear in hot pan for 2 minutes on each side (for rare). Serve with whipped potatoes and drizzle with ponzu sauce.

For the Whipped Potatoes

3 russet potatoes
½ cup cream

1 stick butter
salt and pepper to taste

BOIL potatoes, whip with cream and butter, season to taste.

For the Ponzu Sauce

1 cup mirin
¼ cup soy
⅓ cup ponzu (Japanese lemon/lime dipping sauce available at Oriental markets)

REDUCE mirin by one-quarter. Remove from heat. Add soy and ponzu. Stir. Set aside.

Serves 4

Wine suggestion: a nice Spanish Rioja or Chalone Pinot Noir

CHILI ENCRUSTED DIVER SEA SCALLOPS

Ingredients

12 diver scallops
1 habanero chili pepper
1 bunch cilantro, chopped
2 garlic cloves, crushed
    salt and pepper to taste

1 tablespoon red chili powder
    oil
    toasted pumpkin seeds
    Black Beans (recipe follows)
    Fresh Tomato Salsa (recipe follows)

Preparation

MAKE the black beans and tomato salsa. Combine 2 cups of the reserved black bean liquid with chili pepper, cilantro, and cloves and reduce by half. Strain and puree with ¼ cup black beans, season with salt and pepper to taste.

DUST diver scallops with red chili powder. Pan sear in hot pan for about two minutes per side. Serve on top of rice and black bean combination. Drizzle with black bean sauce. Top scallops with toasted pumpkin seeds and fresh tomato salsa.

For the Fresh Tomato Salsa

2 ripe tomatoes, diced
1 tablespoon onion, diced
1 tablespoon jalapeno, diced

1 tablespoon cilantro, chopped
    salt and pepper
    juice of ½ a lime

MIX together, season to taste.

For the Black Beans

2 cups black beans
    water to cover
2 gallons water

1 tablespoon salt and pepper
1 cup rice, cooked

COVER black beans with water and bring to boil. Drain and discard water. Cover black beans again with two gallons water and cook until tender (approximately one hour). Drain beans, season to taste, and reserve liquid for use in main recipe. Mix 1 cup black beans with 1 cup rice for serving. Any remaining beans can be used in other recipes.

Serves 4

Wine suggestion: Peachy Canyon Zinfandel or Merryvale Sauvignon Blanc

ALMOND AND PANKO CRUSTED CHICKEN BREAST
With Amaretto Cream Sauce

Ingredients

4 6-ounce skinless chicken breasts
1 egg
½ cup water
¼ cup flour

1 cup panko bread crumbs
½ cup sliced almonds
1-2 teaspoons olive oil
Amaretto Cream Sauce (recipe follows)

Preparation

COMBINE egg and water for egg wash. Dredge chicken breast in flour, then in egg wash. Mix bread crumbs with almonds and crust the chicken with bread crumb mixture. Heat sauté pan with olive oil and brown one side of chicken breasts. Turn over and finish in 400-degree oven for 8 minutes.

TO SERVE, place chicken breast on plate and spoon amaretto cream sauce over top.

For Amaretto Cream Sauce

½ cup chicken stock
½ cup cranberry juice
2 cups heavy cream
½ cup Amaretto

½ cup dried cranberries
salt and pepper
roux for thickening

TO MAKE sauce, combine chicken stock, cranberry juice, and heavy cream and bring to a boil. Add Amaretto and reduce by one-quarter volume. Add dried cranberries, salt, and pepper to taste and thicken slightly with roux.

Serves 4

Wine suggestion: Cake Bread Sauvignon Blanc or Echelon Syrah

FILET MIGNON
with Gorgonzola and Port Sauce

Ingredients

4 8-ounce filet tenderloins
½ cup Ficklin port
1 cup beef stock

½ cup Gorgonzola crumbles
   salt and pepper

Preparation

IN A heavy skillet, cook filets on all sides until medium rare (about 7 minutes per side). Remove from pan and deglaze pan with port. Add stock and reduce by one half. Add Gorgonzola crumbles and stir until dissolved. Sauce should coat the back of a spoon. Season with salt and pepper. Pour sauce over filet and top with more Gorgonzola crumbles. Goes well with whipped potatoes and your choice of vegetable.

Serves 4

Wine suggestion: Cain Cuvee or Liberty School Cabernet Sauvignon

Nico's Catacombs

115 South College Avenue
Fort Collins, CO 80524
970-482-6426

Monday - Saturday
5:00 pm to 10:00 pm
Closed Sunday

Nico's Catacombs
Nico and Atie Zentveld, owners/proprietors
Toby Sheppard, chef/co-owner

Opened in May of 1973, by Nico Zentveld and his wife Atie, Nico's Catacombs has become one of the finest restaurants in Colorado and the West. The Catacombs is located in the lower level of the historic Trimble building, which was built in 1905 in downtown Fort Collins. Thousands of wine corks are tastefully arranged on the ceilings and walls. Nico has created a warm bistro atmosphere from a personal greeting by Nico or his wife Atie, to the comfortable chairs and outstanding service. Nico's features over 5,000 different wines from all over the world, and has received the coveted "Best of Award" from the Wine Spectator. The restaurant was also voted "Best Special Occasion Restaurant& Best Wine List" by the readers of The Coloradoan Newspaper for the last 20 years.

Nico's chef and co-owner Toby Sheppard creates sumptuous dishes with a continental flavor. Filet mignon with béarnaise sauce, rack of lamb Chateaubriand, veal Oscar, Dover sole and lobster tail are just a sample of Toby's selections. The creative appetizer menu includes oysters Rockefeller, carpaccio, escargot, and crab cakes. One of the dining highlights is the tableside preparation of dishes as Caesar Salad, Steak Diane, Bananas Megrita, Strawberries Romanoff, Baked Alaska, Café Diablo, and others.

Nico's is well known for their fabulous Winemaker dinners at which the vineyard owners and winemakers visit the restaurant with their wines and Nico and Toby serve a special

Toby and Monica.

five-course dinner paired to the wines. You can finish off your meal in the lounge with a selection of fine brandies or single malt scotches. The classy bar is dominated by one of the most beautiful wine displays you're likely to see anywhere in the world. Behind large etched glass windows is a temperature controlled wine cellar, showing off their award winning selection of wines. Nico's Catacombs is a must for a truly memorable dining experience.

Best of Award of Excellence

Swiss Onion Soup

Ingredients

3 onions, sliced across grain
½ stick butter
6 cups water
1 tablespoon beef base
2 tablespoons chicken base
1 tablespoon fresh thyme
1 bay leaf (with thyme in cheesecloth)
¾ teaspoon white pepper

⅓ cup sherry
⅓ cup Madeira
   roux (enough to thicken)
½ cup heavy cream
½ cup Half and Half
1¼ cups Gruyere, grated (or other high
   quality Swiss cheese)
   salt and pepper to taste

Preparation

SAUTÉ onions in butter. In separate pan, reduce sherry and Madeira by half and set aside. Meanwhile, bring water to a boil in large stockpot along with beef base, chicken base, herbs, and pepper. Set aside. Add onions to boiling broth. Simmer for an hour. Strain out onions into another large stockpot and set aside.

ADD sherry and Madeira to broth, and thicken with roux until it's a little thinner than the final desired consistency. Simmer for half an hour. Bring cream and Half and Half to a boil and add to thickened broth. Gradually stir in grated cheese. When it's well blended, strain into the other pot with the onions and mix well. Adjust seasonings as needed.

Serves 10

Wine suggestion: Geyser Peak, Alexander Valley Reserve Chardonnay

RACK OF LAMB

Ingredients

2 whole 8-bone Colorado lamb racks, split

¼ cup clarified butter or oil

4 tablespoons Dijon mustard
Bread Crumb Mixture (recipe follows)

Preparation

PREHEAT oven to 500 degrees. Clean the lamb racks of excess fat and french the bones (remove all fat and meat from the rib bones). Cut into 4-bone racks. Put a slit in the bottom of the racks so they will stand up when served. Heat a large sauté pan and add the butter. Sear the racks, fat side down, until browned. Stand the lamb upright and finish searing for a minute or so. Remove from sauté pan and stand racks upright on a sheet pan. Spread 1 tablespoon of Dijon mustard on the browned fat of each lamb. Sprinkle bread crumb mixture over the mustard. Cover the bones of each rack with aluminum foil. Be sure there is enough foil to loosely cover the bread crumb-topped portion of lamb racks. Roast in 500 degree oven for approximately 20 minutes.

For the Bread Crumb Mixture

1 cup bread crumbs
½ cup Parmesan cheese
1 tablespoon oregano
1 tablespoon basil

1 teaspoon black pepper
1 teaspoon garlic
1 tablespoon fresh mint

MIX together and set aside until needed.

Serves 4

Wine Suggestion: Silver Oak, Napa Cabernet Sauvignon, 1998

ENTRECÔTE AU POIVRE (PEPPER STEAK)

Ingredients

14 ounces New York steak, trimmed and
  butterflied
 2 tablespoons whole butter
½ cup bordelaise sauce
 2 tablespoons brandy
¼ cup beef stock

Pernod liqueur, dash
Tabasco, dash
Worcestershire sauce, dash
¼ teaspoon dry mustard
¼ cup heavy cream

Preparation

HEAT a sauté pan and add the butter. Add the steak, butterflied side down. (This side will be served up) Sear this side and remove from pan. Deglaze the pan with a touch of the bordelaise sauce, then flame with the brandy. Add the remainder of the sauce, then the beef stock. Add a few dashes of Pernod, Tabasco and Worcestershire, and the dry mustard. Finish with cream, add the steak back to the sauce, and cook to desired doneness.

Serves 1

Wine suggestion: Rosemount Shiraz, "Balmoral", 1999

Nico's wine cellar.

Nico's dining room.

Nico's Catacombs, Fort Collins

RASPBERRY TRUFFLES

Ingredients

19 ounces semi-sweet chocolate chips
1 cup heavy cream
½ cup raspberry puree
2 tablespoons Chambord liqueur

chocolate for coating
clarified butter
white chocolate chips

Preparation

HEAT cream to boiling, and then cool slightly and set aside. Fill sauce pan with hot water, put chocolate chips in mixing bowl and using mixing bowl as a double boiler, melt part way. Add cream and melt until smooth, then add puree and Chambord. Beat until mixed well, then put the bowl back into the saucepan of water and cool in refrigerator until set, then mix again, cool, mix etc. until proper consistency. Roll into 1-ounce balls on wire rack. Coat with melted chocolate (chocolate chips and clarified butter), then garnish with stripes of white chocolate.

Makes 24 balls

Black Bear Restaurant

Black Bear
Restaurant

10375 Ute Pass Rd.
P.O. Box 132
Green Mt. Falls, CO 80819
719-684-9648
www.blackbearrestaurant.com

Tuesday-Sunday
Bar 2 pm - close
Dining Room 5 pm – close
Closed Monday

Black Bear Restaurant
Victor Matthews, Chef-Owner

Chef-Owner Victor Matthews is a unique individual; an award-winning chef with a business ability to match. He has taken a log cabin restaurant built in 1959 in Green Mountain Falls, a town of only 800 people, and turned it into an outstanding dining experience that appeals to the fine cuisine aficionado as well as the local resident who loves a gathering place with good food and good company.

The lounge retains its rustic atmosphere from the establishment that preceded Chef Matthews' venture, but as you step into the dining room you are amazed at the beautiful chandeliers, crisp white linen cloths and sparkling wine glasses. The fabulous river rock fireplace adds a special warmth and coziness to the room.

Victor Matthews is a chef who has gone through the rigors of a classic 7-year apprenticeship in the true European tradition. He trained under some of the finest Master Chefs in the world in the early 90's in New Orleans, earning his designation as Chef in 1995.

Chef Matthews calls his cuisine Nuevo Colorado, a very eclectic mix of styles, using a great deal of special Colorado products and farm produce. He has Italian, French, Southern, Cajun Creole, New American, Indian, Japanese, Chinese, Southwestern and even Caribbean influences in his creations. It is a delight to find such ingredients as Kobe and Piedmontese beef, Foie Gras, artisan cheeses, fresh truffles, and homemade prosciutto, in such a setting, not to mention live lobsters at 8,000 feet.

The chef's philosophy is to find local fresh ingredients and intensify their natural flavors, not masking them with too many "trendy" sauces and flavors. His classical training has taught him to "take the absolute best ingredients, almost never make menus ahead of time, and create ala minute, on the spot masterpieces based upon the strength of ultra-fresh and creative ingredients." This approach has created a culinary reputation that bears itself out in the dining room every night. Usually, as many as half of the tables are chef's tables; all with different menus.

As Chef Matthews is known for saying, "You gotta try this!"

Victor Matthews

Black Bear Restaurant, Green Mountain Falls

214

Wapiti Roulade Canapés

Wapiti, or Rocky Mountain Regional Elk, is the center of this dish, but there are several complex techniques that need to be employed. The first is "farce", which is simply a forcemeat made from the elk trimming, herbs and vegetables. This will constitute part of the stuffing. Also we will need a duxelle, which is a cooked down mushroom puree, and a few large white asparagus.

Ingredients

1 elk loin	2 cups wild mushrooms, finely diced
½ small carrot, chopped	1½ tablespoons of shallot
½ small onion, chopped	1 teaspoon garlic
½ small celery stalk, chopped	1-2 tablespoons olive oil
salt	3 bay leaves
pepper	½ cup good red wine
fresh herbs, such as thyme and basil	2 spears thick white asparagus, trimmed
1 egg	10 layers of phyllo dough
1 tablespoon tomato paste	2 tablespoons butter, melted
1 teaspoon paprika	1 egg
1 tablespoon roasted garlic, finely minced	1 tablespoon granulated garlic
	sprig thyme

Preparation

TRIM an elk loin to just the beautiful center loin meat. To make farce, take the meat scraps and what little fat you may have and puree along with the chopped carrot, onion, and celery, a pinch of salt and pepper, and a small bunch of fresh herbs. Add egg to this mix along with tomato paste, paprika, and roasted garlic. Mix until smooth. Refrigerate your farce.

TO MAKE duxelle, sauté wild mushrooms with shallot and garlic in olive oil in a sauté pan. Add bay leaves and red wine, along with a pinch of salt and pepper. Cook this down, reducing the entire lot on medium low till it is completely dry. This takes a while. Remove bay leaves and refrigerate your duxelle.

TAKE well-trimmed elk loin and slice it slowly down the middle at an angle while rolling it out. This takes practice, but you are "opening it up". Take your time. You should end up with a flat wide rectangle of elk less than half an inch thick.

LIGHTLY poach the asparagus spears in salted water…and I mean lightly, like two minutes. Shock in ice water and refrigerate your asparagus. Butter and stack at least ten layers of phyllo. Save under a moist towel until ready. When ready to assemble the entire dish, remove towel and coat the entire phyllo heavily with butter and egg wash.

WAPITI ROULADE CANAPÉS
CONTINUED

LAY the flattened open elk onto the phyllo. Season with salt and pepper and a bit of granulated garlic and thyme.

SPREAD a layer of farce onto elk trying to keep it the same thickness all around.

REFRIGERATE or freeze just till stiff. Spread a layer of duxelle on top of farce. Careful not to mix them, and keep them cold. Line up asparagus lengthwise near edge and cut to fit if necessary. Roll up the entire roulade. Result should be a tight roll with white asparagus in the center and lines of brown duxelle and red farce swirling with the pastry.

REFRIGERATE entire roll to firm and keep round.

FINALLY, bake for 20 minutes at 450 degrees and let stand for ten minutes.

CAREFULLY cut half-inch thick pinwheels and serve as a warm or cold canapé.

ALTERNATELY, you can semi-freeze the roll and cut the pinwheels ahead of time, baking them to order. They won't look as neat, but they will be easier to cut, and hotter, if those are concerns. This is, of course, also servable as an entrée for one or more depending on loin size.

Serve as canapés or entree

WILD MUSHROOM POLENTA WITH TRUFFLE OIL

Polenta is a beautiful and versatile dish originating in Northern Italy. I suppose I fell in love with it early on because it seemed like the advanced fine dining version of grits, one of the favorite dishes of my youth in the American South. Italians however, have taken cornmeal to a whole new level of complexity and functionality. This dish can be served hot and soft, warm and slightly firm, or cool and completely firm. In the latter case, we would carve it into squares or triangles and could either eat it cold or pan fry it to re-warm. There are few dishes as versatile as polenta. In essence, it is just cornmeal. In fact, I have made great polenta with simple cornmeal from a supermarket bag. However, we always prefer a larger stone-ground grain when possible. It takes longer to cook but absorbs more flavor and yields much more nutrition. In general, polenta can be bought instant or completely raw. Again, the instant cooks very quickly and is convenient, but the longer cooking version tastes better and is much better for you.

There are two approaches to polenta. The first is to cook it plain, just salted water, and then add sauces later; treating it sort of like pasta. The second is to add it to well-seasoned stock, creating a finished product. This treatment is more like risotto. Either will do, but this recipe uses the second version.

Ingredients

1 onion, fine minced	3 bay leaves
2 cloves of garlic, fine minced	2 cups chicken stock
1-3 tablespoons of olive oil	1 cup of polenta
3 portobello mushrooms, diced	salt and pepper to taste
3 shiitake mushrooms, diced	¼ cup Parmesan
1 cup of white wine	1 tablespoon butter
2 sprigs of thyme	1 teaspoon white truffle oil

Preparation

KEEP in mind that exact liquid amounts vary dramatically from one polenta to another. Always have a little extra stock to add if it gets too thick before it is soft. A large grain organic product takes about three to one ratio, but it could be as low as one to one, or as high as five to one. Three or four to one is always a good guess.

SAUTÉ onion and garlic in olive oil. Add mushrooms and sauté longer. Deglaze with white wine. Bring to a boil. Add seasonings, herbs, and stock. Boil softly five minutes to complete "mushroom stock". Add polenta in a slow "rain" while stirring continuously. Stir, stir, stir. No lumps. Cook on low, always stirring, for at least 20 minutes, until it is soft and done. Finish with Parmesan and butter. Serve hot, or pour onto a board and cool. For an elegant modern taste, add a drizzle of white truffle oil. Useable at least two or three days in a row.

Serves 1-2

TORPEDO PORK AND MELON FROM THE GRILL
with Tangerine Honey

Ingredients

pork chops or pork loin
melon, such as cantaloupe, honey
dew, etc.

honey, good quality
tangerine concentrate (optional)

THIS is an unbelievably easy and delicious, but rarely attempted, summertime recipe. All you need is your favorite pork for the grill (I use Nick Mauro's Torpedo Pork from his farm in Pueblo, available at all local farmer's markets). Normally, I use chops, but you can do this with pork loin if you like.

GET your favorite melon, nice and ripe, and slice it up. These pieces should be large enough that they won't fall through the grill. I like the standard half-moon style slices. Finally, some good honey. Regular honey works fine. Organic local honey works better (again, available at farmer's markets), and some form of flavored honey is even better. Glenn Austin's local organic honey from his peach orchard, that's my favorite of all. You can get a million kinds, from orange blossom to lavender, and they are all great, OR, you can make your own. Take a concentrate from something you love (in this case we used Tangerine concentrate) and puree a little bit in the blender with your honey (room temperature). This will scent the honey and it will last several weeks at least in the fridge.

That's it.

FIRE up the grill and get good marks on your fruit and pork. Lightly salt and pepper, and add just a tiny sprinkle of sugar if your fruit isn't fully ripe. Pile it up on a plate (decorate however you feel), and drizzle with the honey. Enjoy!

By the way, a great chilled Riesling or Gewürztraminer would go great with this, especially on a warm day outside. I recommend Colorado Riesling like Two Rivers or Plum Creek.

Brinegar's Spaghetti

This is my grandma's spaghetti recipe. This is the best spaghetti in the world…it is crazy how good it is, and the flavors are a little more complex than standard greasy attempts at meat sauce.

Grandma Rose had a huge farm in the mountains of North Carolina and a cellar bigger than a modern restaurant's. We had a natural spring on the farm, bees, and every form of livestock and garden you can imagine. Grandma's Sunday dinners were legendary. Dozens of family members and friends would come by and sit on the porch and throw down the best cuisine any of us had ever seen. I ate more of this spaghetti than I care to admit, half of it in the middle of the night and cold, but it was just that good.

I still can't beat this spaghetti. It is taken from a torn old faded sheet of paper in her scribble - it's simple, non-traditional, and countrified, but it was my first glimpse of the possible greatness of cuisine.

Ingredients

1½ pounds hamburger	salt
2 cups sharp cheese, grated	pepper
1 large chopped onion	5-6 slices of bacon, cut small
½ green pepper, chopped	1 small and 1 large can tomato soup
2 eggs	2 cans tomato paste
1-2 slices of bread, wet	1 large can tomato sauce
1 teaspoon caraway seeds	mushrooms, cut up
1 tablespoon sugar	garlic, cut up
1 tablespoon parsley	spaghetti noodles

Preparation

COMBINE cheese, onion, pepper, eggs, bread, caraway seeds, sugar, parsley, salt, and pepper. Mix into hamburger and form into meatballs.

FRY bacon pieces in very large skillet, then brown meatballs in bacon fat. Combine soup, tomato paste, tomato sauce, mushrooms, and garlic in a very large pot. Drain most of fat from meatballs and bacon and then place in large pot with the sauce.

COOK slowly - between 4-6 hours. A crock-pot works well for this.

Enjoy!!!!

Serves 4-6

Pikes Peak or Bust Rodeo, Colorado Springs. (1968)

Briarhurst Manor

404 Manitou Avenue
Manitou Springs, CO 80829
719-685-1864
www.briarhurst.com

Sunday – Saturday
5:00 pm – 9:00 pm

Briarhurst Manor
Lawrence "Chip" Johnson, Executive Chef

Listed on the National Historic Registry, Briarhurst Manor is a true adventure for the Western history buff that also enjoys fine dining. Located in the tiny valley of Manitou Springs at the foot of Pike's Peak, the pink sandstone manor was originally built in 1876 by the founder of Manitou Springs, Dr. William Bell. Dr. Bell and his wife, Cara, built the manor to resemble the fine English country houses that they both loved from their native England. The name Briarhurst was taken because of William and Cara's love of the wild rose bushes that grew on the property. They reminded the couple of the sweetbriar that grew in England. Dr. Bell figured prominently in the early history Colorado, founding the Denver & Rio Grande Railroad with his friend, General William Palmer,

In 1886, burning embers from a fireplace destroyed the interior of the manor, causing the Bells to lose almost all their belongings, but no loss of lives among the children and servants. In the spring of 1887, the Bells began the work of reconstructing the manor to an even grander scale. The manor became the social center of the community, as William and Cara hosted many famous national and international names.

Today, the manor remains much as originally envisioned, with 12 unique fireplaces, and 12 main rooms showcasing fine woodworking. A walking tour of the first 2 floors of the manor is available, and the estate makes a perfect romantic setting for weddings.

In 1974, Sigi Krauss opened Briarhurst as a fine restaurant. Today, Ken Healey continues the reputation for fine food. And has re-created an atmosphere that brings back memories of life as the Bell's knew it in the early West. The friendly staff is eager to share the history of the estate and answer any questions about Briarhurst Manor.

Chef Lawrence "Chip" Johnson joined the staff as Executive Chef in 2001. His interest in food began as a child, and his culinary education has led him to serve as chef and restaurant manager in some of the premier Colorado establishments. His early enjoyment of hunting and preparing wild game shows in the wide selection of tempting game dishes on the menu, such as Colorado Elk Loin with Merlot-Blackberry Demiglace and Mountain Mushroom Ragout or Four Corners Boar, Served with Green Chili Sauce and Red Chili Crepes. The menu is also replete with domestic dishes featuring fresh Pacific Coast salmon, prime grass-fed aged Colorado beef, and Colorado lamb.

CASHEW CRUSTED CRAB
with Strawberry-Horseradish Emulsion
appetizer

This appetizer recreates the flavors of Port Baltimore in the 1800's. The idea for this appetizer originated from the practice that Chesapeake Bay fishermen had of using horseradish medicinally to prevent influenza and to cure colds. These fishermen discovered that the addition of honey and berries to the horseradish made this concoction sweeter and much easier to ingest. The idea of using this flavor combination, along with the easy availability of abundant amounts of fresh crabmeat, enticed local chefs to experiment. The personal touch that we bring to this dish is to encrust the crab with a natural match of salty cashews, perfectly complimenting the sweet, tangy sauce.

Ingredients

3 pounds fresh Maryland jumbo lump blue crab
2 cups mayonnaise
5 tablespoons mustard
2 tablespoons Old Bay seasoning
2 tablespoons fresh chopped parsley
1 tablespoon fresh chopped cilantro
½ teaspoon ground white pepper
½ teaspoon dry mustard
½ ounce malt vinegar
1 ounce dry sherry
1 teaspoon Tabasco sauce
2 cups panko (Japanese bread crumbs)
2 cups beaten whole eggs
2 cups roasted cashews, minced
Strawberry-Horseradish Emulsion (recipe follows)
Wasabi Cream (recipe follows)

Preparation

IN A large mixing bowl, combine the mayonnaise, mustard, seasonings, herbs, vinegar, and sherry. Blend well and then stir in the crabmeat and the Tabasco sauce.

FOLD in the panko until mixture is moist throughout. Shape the crab mix into cakes.

DIP the crab cakes in beaten egg and then roll them in minced cashews.

TO SERVE, sauté the crab cakes in butter over medium heat until golden brown.

LADLE a pool of the strawberry emulsion onto a serving plate. Drizzle with a small amount of the wasabi cream and swirl with a toothpick or knife tip. Arrange the crab cakes on the plate and garnish as desired.

CASHEW CRUSTED CRAB
CONTINUED

For the Strawberry-Horseradish Emulsion

2 ounces port wine
1 cup strawberry preserves
5 tablespoons horseradish pulp

1 ounce unsalted butter
1 ounce olive oil
1 quart fresh strawberries, sliced

IN A large saucepan, reduce the port wine by half. Add the preserves, horseradish, butter, and olive oil. Simmer for about 1 hour, blend well, and then incorporate the fresh berries into this emulsion.

For the Wasabi Cream

1 ounce wasabi powder
1 ounce water

1 ounce Tasmanian honey
½ cup mayonnaise

COMBINE all ingredients in small mixing bowl and blend thoroughly.

Serves 8

REDMESA BARBECUED DOUBLECHOPS OF COLORADO LAMB
with Grilled Vegetables and Blue Corn Chappatis

This recipe is easily done in the home kitchen, and it is simple to prepare the different elements of this dish ahead of time so it can be quickly finished off when you are ready to start grilling. I started this dish by thinking about what I feel would best represent the all-round flavors of Colorado. I thought lamb would be a great way to show what I like the most about modern Colorado foods: involved and caring ranchers, superior products, and great taste. Then I added a bit of the historical flavors that have influenced Colorado dishes for so many years: chilies, tomatoes, peppers, and a variety of southwestern spices. I added some Colorado raised vegetables, because grilled vegetables have a delicious and unique flavor. I then finished off this dish by adding a historically authentic flatbread, one whose history can be traced back to the beginning of bread making.

Ingredients

8 double cut Colorado lamb chops
1½ cups apple cider
1 cinnamon stick
¼ cup mild salsa
2 crushed garlic cloves
1 bay leaf
1 teaspoon cracked black peppercorns
2 teaspoons kosher salt
1 teaspoon mustard powder

assorted vegetables, such as corn, carrots, fava beans, baby squashes, tomatillos, new potatoes or baby tomatoes
salt, pepper, basil or sage to taste
Redmesa Barbecue Sauce (recipe follows)
Blue Corn Chappatis (recipe follows)

Preparation

COMBINE apple cider, cinnamon stick, salsa, garlic cloves, bay leaf, black peppercorns, salt, and mustard powder to make marinade. Marinate lamb chops for 20-30 minutes.

PREPARE the Redmesa Barbecue Sauce and the Blue Corn Chappatis.

COOK the vegetables in a mesh grill basket, keeping the seasoning light, as there is plenty of flavor on the plate already. A little salt, pepper, and maybe a bit of finely cut basil and sage work well. While the vegetables cook, drizzle them with some of the barbeque sauce for a unique flavor.

TO COOK lamb, heat a grill (preferably charcoal) to a high heat. Remove the lamb from the marinade and place it on the grill. Turn the chops so that all sides are seared quickly, and then reduce the grill heat to low. Baste the chops with a thick coat of the barbeque sauce and cover the grill. Keep the heat low and baste the lamb chops thoroughly with the barbeque sauce every 5 to 10 minutes throughout the cooking process. We prefer to serve our lamb medium rare to medium, which usually takes about 15 to 20 minutes. Give the lamb one final thick basting right before serving.

TO SERVE, place lamb, blue corn chappatis, and roasted vegetables on plate and enjoy!

For the Redmesa Barbecue Sauce

1 cup apple cider
2 tablespoons red chili powder
1 Fresno pepper, minced
1 jalapeno pepper, minced
¼ cup green chili, diced
2 garlic cloves, crushed
1 cup red tomato, diced

2 tablespoons tomato paste
¼ cup white onion, minced
¼ cup honey
½ teaspoon cumin
1 teaspoon coriander
  Pinch of ground clove
3 ounces dark chocolate, chopped

REDMESA BARBECUED DOUBLECHOPS OF COLORADO LAMB
with Grilled Vegetables and Blue Corn Chappatis
CONTINUED

COMBINE all of the above ingredients in a saucepan, bring to a low boil, reduce the heat, and simmer for about a half hour. Be sure to stir frequently.

For the Blue Corn Chappatis

1 cup blue cornmeal	1 tablespoon olive oil
1 cup white flour	1 tablespoon minced parsley
½ teaspoon salt	1 tablespoon mustard seed
¾ cup water	1 tablespoon minced red pepper

IN A mixing bowl, combine the cornmeal, flour, and salt and mix well. Make a well in the center and add the oil and water. Mix the flour into the liquid and knead. Add the parsley, mustard seed, and red pepper. Knead until all ingredients are well mixed. The dough should be smooth and elastic. Set the dough aside and allow it to rest for at least 15 minutes, but not more than 45 minutes. Form the dough into plum sized balls, then flatten the balls on a floured board until very thin, in a circle about 4" in diameter. Place the chappatis on an area of the grill that is not too hot and cook until bubbles begin to form on the surface. Flip the chappatis over and cook for only about 20 to 30 more seconds. Place cooked chappatis in a napkin-lined basket and cover; be sure to serve warm.

Serves 4

This dish goes very well with a good, hearty Pinot Noir.

SICILIAN PHEASANT

Ingredients

2 tablespoons olive oil
1 tablespoon butter
1 tablespoon garlic, chopped
6 boneless, wing-on 8-ounce pheasant
    breasts
    kosher salt
    fresh ground black pepper
    flour

3 large red tomatoes, diced
3 large yellow tomatoes, diced
1 tablespoon fresh basil chiffonade
3 tablespoons whole fresh tarragon
    leaves
⅓ cup kalamata olives, sliced
1½ cups Chablis

Preparation

HEAT sauté pan to high heat. Carefully add the olive oil, butter, and chopped garlic. Allow the garlic to brown and become slightly sticky. Season the pheasant breasts with salt and pepper, dredge heavily in flour, and place skin side down in the sauté pan. Cook until the skin is brown and crispy. Turn the breasts over and add the tomatoes, herbs and olives to the pan, shake the sauté pan to spread out the ingredients, and then add the Chablis. Place in a 350 degree oven and leave until the breasts are just cooked through. Place the breasts on a serving plate and reduce the seasoned tomatoes to desired consistency. Adjust salt and pepper and pour the tomatoes over the cooked pheasant breasts.

Serves 6

This dish goes very well with most medium bodied Chardonnays. Look for a wine with good, crisp fruit tones.

ROULADE OF REINDEER
with Cranberry Chutney

Ingredients

3 pounds reindeer leg meat
   salad oil
2½ tablespoons fresh garlic, minced
   salt and pepper
2 bunches fresh spinach leaves
4 red peppers, roasted and cut into
   strips

1 bunch fresh basil leaves
   wild rice, cooked
1 cup pinion nuts, toasted
8 slices bacon
   Cranberry Chutney (recipe follows)

Preparation

SLICE reindeer leg meat into five-ounce portions. Lay the sliced meat portions on a cutting board, cover with plastic wrap and lightly pound the meat with the flat side of a mallet, slowly working the edges out. Do this until the slices have been evenly spread out to about ¼" thickness. Remove the plastic wrap and rub entire surface of the meat with a light coat of salad oil and minced fresh garlic. Sprinkle with salt and pepper. Lay down a layer of fresh spinach leaves, then strips of roasted red pepper and then a layer of fresh basil leaves. Finish with a layer of cooked wild rice and a sprinkle of toasted pinion nuts. Cover the roulades with plastic wrap and roll flat with a rolling pin. Remove the plastic wrap and carefully roll the roulades as tightly as possible. Fully wrap each roulade with a slice of bacon. Cook in a 350 degree oven until the roulades have reached an internal temperature of 120 degrees. Remove from the oven and allow to rest for about 5 minutes, then slice into thin medallions. Arrange the medallions on a serving plate and drizzle with the cranberry chutney.

For the Cranberry Chutney

1 pound whole cranberries
¼ teaspoon ground cloves
   pinch of cayenne
2 tablespoons raspberry vinegar
1 cup Major Grey's chutney

½ cup brown sugar
1 tablespoon orange zest
¼ teaspoon limejuice
½ cup port wine
   cornstarch and water to thicken

COMBINE all of the above ingredients in a saucepan and bring to low boil. Reduce the heat and simmer for about a half hour. Thicken slightly, if necessary, with a small amount of cornstarch slurry.

Serves 8

We like to serve this dish with a good Colorado produced Cabernet Sauvignon, preferably from Cottonwood Cellars.

Briarhurst Manor, Manitou Springs

INDIAN BUTTER CREAM APRICOTS
with Nougat Sauce and Apple-Port Shimmer

This is a favorite fall dessert of Chef Chip Johnson's. It's a great follow up after a dinner of wild game. He says even though it looks complicated, it's easy to do, and makes you look like a master chef.

Ingredients

25 apricots
3 gallons water
6 cups sugar
1 teaspoon allspice
1 teaspoon clove

¼ cup lemon juice
Butter Cream (recipe follows)
Nougat Sauce (recipe follows)
Apple-Port Shimmer (recipe follows)

Preparation

START the day before to make the vanilla sauce, which is part of the nougat sauce. The day you plan to serve the dessert, make the butter cream sauce, the nougat sauce, and the apple-port shimmer.

TO PREPARE the apricots, make the poaching liquid by combining water, sugar, allspice, clove, and lemon juice. Heat to boiling.

IMMERSE the apricots in the boiling liquid, turn down to a simmer, and poach for 8-10 minutes, until apricots are tender. Dry on baking rack until cool. Once the apricots are cool, pull the seeds out using a pair of needle nose pliers. Fill each apricot with butter cream.

TO SERVE, spoon a small amount of the nougat sauce onto a serving plate so it forms a pool. Place an apricot in the center of the plate and drizzle with the apple-port shimmer sauce.

GARNISH as desired.

For the Butter Cream

32 egg yolks
4 vanilla beans
2 cups water

2 cups sugar
3 pounds unsalted butter, room temperature

BEAT egg yolks until thick, lemon colored and ribboning. Add seeds from vanilla beans. Combine the sugar and water and bring to a 250-degree boil. Beat the hot sugar into the egg yolks, continue beating until cool, then gradually beat in the butter.

INDIAN BUTTER CREAM APRICOTS
with Nougat Sauce and Apple-Port Shimmer
CONTINUED

For the Nougat Sauce

30 egg yolks
2 cups sugar
1 cup honey
3 quarts heavy cream

2 tablespoons vanilla extract
4 cups shelled, roasted hazelnuts
4 cups sugar
¼ cup water

THE day before, make the vanilla sauce. Combine the egg yolks, sugar, honey, heavy cream and vanilla extract and heat until the mixture starts to coat the side of the mixing bowl. Pour through a chinois into a storage container and refrigerate overnight before using.

COMBINE sugar and water and bring to a medium boil, cook until sugar mixture turns a golden color, about 10 minutes. Spread hazelnuts out on a sheetpan, pour the sugar mixture over the nuts, and allow to cool until hard. Put in a food processor and pulse until well chopped. Stir into 4 cups of the vanilla sauce.

For the Apple-Port Shimmer

1 cup apple butter
1 cup apple concentrate

1 cup apple juice
1 cup port

IF YOU can't find apple concentrate, simply increase the apple butter to two cups. Combine all ingredients in a small saucepan. Bring to a simmer and whisk well. Serve warm over the top of the prepared apricots.

Serves 25

This dessert is excellent with most tawny ports.

Cliff House

306 Canon Avenue
Manitou Springs,
Colorado 80829
888-212-7000
719-685-3000
www.thecliffhouse.com

Seven days a week
6:30 am- 10:30 am
11:30 am – 2:30 pm
5:30 pm – 9:00 pm

The Cliff House at Pikes Peak

Built in the winter of 1873, the Cliff House in Manitou Springs has been serving guests longer than Colorado has been a state. The Manitou Springs have bubbled up from the underground limestone aquifers for centuries, and many believe the refreshing mineral-infused water has healing powers.

Gold mines brought people to the Pikes Peak area in the late 1850s, and the town of Manitou Springs was born. The 20-room boarding house known as "The Inn" began as a stagecoach stop along the route from Colorado Springs to Leadville. This was one of the most famous stagecoach runs of the American West. The trappers and hunters, traveling to or from Colorado Springs, spent time relaxing in the pleasant parlors or on the sprawling porches.

Over the years, the hotel expanded from 20 rooms to 200, resulting in the beautiful, four-and-a-half story building that still stands today.

The Cliff House was a destination for the wealthy, and guests included Theodore Roosevelt, Ferdinand-Crown Prince of Austria, William Henry Jackson, Charles Dickens Jr., P.T. Barnum, Thomas Edison, Clark Gable, F. W. Woolworth, and J. Paul Getty.

Known for elegance and taste, those themes continue in today's Cliff House, which offers one of the premier dining experiences in Colorado. Surrounded by Victorian scenes in oils by local legend C.H. Rockey, you can dine like a king. Sip from Riedel crystal wine glasses, and sup from Villroy and Boch China, using the Christofle Hotel flatware, while seated on the veranda, gazing at the majestic Rocky Mountains.

The cuisine is Nouveau Continental, and dishes are determined based on seasonal ingredients. The wine list is extensive, with over 700 selections to enhance your meal, distinguished by the Wine Spectator Award of Excellence. Six certified sommeliers, two of which are certified by the Court of Master Sommeliers, are available to assist you. The service is highly trained and attentive.

The experience is unbeatable.

Y Award of Excellence

GOAT CHEESE SOUFFLÉ
appetizer

Ingredients

1¾   ounces butter
⅓   cup flour
1⅓ cups milk
 4   egg yolks
 1   teaspoon Dijon mustard
 4   ounces Chèvre goat cheese
 1   teaspoon chives

½   teaspoon thyme
1   teaspoon Italian parsley
1   teaspoon shallot
1   dash Tabasco sauce
1   teaspoon lemon juice
    salt and pepper to taste
6   egg whites

Preparation

MAKE roux with butter and flour and toast on low heat for 3-4 minutes. Incorporate milk slowly. When sauce thickens, simmer for 3 minutes. Whisk in egg yolks and cook for one minute on medium heat. Remove from heat and add all remaining ingredients except egg whites. Allow to stand for 30 minutes.

BUTTER four 8-ounce soufflé ramekins. Whip egg whites to medium stiff peaks, fold into soufflé base gently with a spatula (do not use a whip). Fill soufflé ramekins to just below the rim, and place filled ramekins in a large pan with sides 2 inches high. Put the pan into a 350 degree oven (do not close door to oven). Fill the pan with hot water half way up the sides of the ramekins. Bake at 375 degrees for 20-25 minutes. Remove and let soufflés remain in water bath on the counter for 15 minutes. Take ramekins from the water bath and cool for 20 minutes. Run a paring knife around the rim to loosen and gently invert soufflé into hand, place on a parchment lined sheet tray, then refrigerate.

TO SERVE, reheat soufflé at 350 degrees for 4-5 minutes, serve immediately by itself or on a salad of Belgian endive and baby greens with a drizzle of white truffle oil or the vinaigrette of your choice.

Serves 4

Cliff House Clam Chowder

The most important part of any soup is that everything must be cut the same size. You want to taste it all.

Ingredients

6 cups potatoes, small diced, placed in water
2 cups bacon, chopped
2 cups white onion, chopped
2 cups celery stalks, chopped

1½ pound can chopped clams in juice
2 cups flour
6 cups milk
salt and pepper to taste
parsley for garnish

Preparation

YOU will need two pots for this soup, one for the soup and the other for the potatoes. Have a pot of boiling water on the stove before you start chopping your ingredients. Go ahead and par-cook your potatoes. When they are done, pull them out of the water and run cold water over them. You want them to have a little crunch to them, as they will continue to cook once they are in the soup.

USING a heavy-bottomed soup pot, place on the stove on high heat (the pot should be really hot!) Start by adding your bacon. You need to render off the fat, but the fat is very important part of the soup, so do not discard it. As soon as the bacon looks almost crisp, add the onion and celery. Cook until the vegetables are soft, but still have a little crunch.

WHILE you are waiting for this to happen, open the clams. Strain the clams with a pasta strainer or something similar. Save the juice and rinse the clams under cold water. When your vegetables are ready, add flour, a little at a time. You are making a roux, the thickening agent for the soup. When you are adding the flour to the mixture, it is going to look really thick, almost like a paste. This is what you want, in order to control how thick your soup will be. Add half of the clam juice to the soup slowly and whisk. Try to keep the soup at a warm temperature at all times so the flour will dissolve easily. Next, add your milk to the soup, slowly. Add the par-cooked potatoes and season with salt and pepper. If the soup needs more clam flavor, add the rest of the clam juice. Garnish with parsley.

Serves 8-10

BALSAMIC BRAISED LAMB SHANK

Ingredients

4   16-20 ounce choice lamb shanks
2   cups carrots, medium diced
2   cups celery, medium diced
2   cups onion, medium diced
    salt and pepper
    flour
    olive oil
¼   cup aged balsamic vinegar

¼   cup molasses
2   cups red wine
½   cup rich veal stock
    water for braising
2   tablespoons whole thyme
1   tablespoon rosemary
10 garlic cloves
1-4 tablespoons butter

Preparation

MAKE mirepoix by combining carrots, celery, and onion. Clean and french the lamb shanks, leaving a majority of the fat to render. Rub liberally with salt and pepper. Lightly dust with flour.

IN A heavy bottom braising pot, heat oil until slightly smoking. Sear lamb shanks on each side. Reduce heat, add mirepoix, and sauté for two minutes. Add vinegar and reduce by half, add molasses, red wine, and veal stock. Coat lamb with sauce and reduce until sauce coats lamb evenly.

COVER with water. Add herbs, and garlic cloves. Cover pot with heavy foil and braise in a 225 degree oven at least 1½ hours. Meat should be very tender but not falling off of the bone.

STRAIN braising liquid, skim off excess fat and reduce for sauce. Once reduced to desired thickness, season with salt and pepper and add small chunks of cold butter to taste, whisking to blend. Great accompanied by soft polenta and grilled vegetables.

Serves 4

TAMARIND LACQUERED DUCKLING
with Persimmon Coulis and Cellophane Noodle Vegetable Slaw

Ingredients

2   4-pound ducklings
¼   cup grape seed oil
    Brine Solution (recipe follows)
    Confit (recipe follows)
    Tamarind Lacquer (recipe follows)
    Ponzu Sauce (recipe follows)

    Persimmon Coulis (recipe follows)
    Cellophane Noodle and Root
    Vegetable Slaw (recipe follows)
1   tablespoon grape seed oil, for slaw
1   clove garlic, minced, for slaw

Preparation

THE day before, remove the breast, leg, and thigh from the duckling. Place the breast skin side up in the refrigerator for 4-6 hours. Remove all of the skin and fat from the carcass, place in a thick bottom pot, and render fat on low heat, reserve. Make a simple four-quart stock from the duck bones, strain and reduce to 1 cup, reserving for the tamarind lacquer recipe. Make brine solution, place the leg and thigh in the brine solution, and refrigerate overnight.

EARLY on the day the dish is to be served, make the confit, tamarind lacquer, ponzu sauce and persimmon coulis.

WHEN ready to serve, take a very hot, large sauté pan, and add ¼ cup of grape seed oil. Take out the confit legs and make sure all excess fat from the confit is wiped off. When oil has reached the smoking point, carefully place the confit legs in the pan, being careful to drop the legs into the pan away from your body, due to splashing.

SAUTÉ the confit legs 1½ minutes or until skin is crispy and golden. Brown, then flip legs onto the other side. Transfer to ovenproof pan, add duck breasts, skin side down, and place the duck into a 375 degree oven for 8 minutes. While cooking, prepare the ingredients as directed for the cellophane noodle and root vegetable slaw, which will be finished right before serving.

REMOVE from oven and flip to skin side up. Paint liberally with tamarind lacquer and return to the oven for 2 minutes. Remove and allow duck to rest 5-7 minutes before serving.

FOR THE slaw, take a medium saucepan and add minced garlic and tablespoon of grape seed oil. Add beet, carrot, radish, and pepper, sauté until al dente. Add ½ to ¾ cups of the ponzu sauce and toss until incorporated. Add peanuts, cucumber, herbs, and noodles.

TO SERVE, place a small pile for noodle slaw to the back of the plate. Lean the leg up against the slaw. Slice the breast on the bias and fan out in front of the leg. Decorate the plate with the persimmon coulis.

Bon Appetite!

For the Brine Solution

8 cups water	2 bay leaves
¼ cup sugar	1 fresh lime
½ cup salt	1 fresh lemon
1 tablespoon whole peppercorns	4 cups mirepoix

COMBINE all ingredients.

For the Confit

4 duck leg/thigh, from brine solution	2 tablespoons rosemary
2 tablespoons grape seed oil	duck fat to cover meat
4 garlic cloves	

REMOVE duck leg/thigh from brine solution. In a hot sauté pan add 2 tablespoons grape seed oil, place duck leg and thigh skin side down. Sauté until skin is golden brown and crisp. Place duck legs and thighs in an ovenproof casserole dish and add whole garlic, rosemary and rendered duck fat, with the duck fat covering the leg/thighs completely. Bake the confit at 220 degrees for three hours and then set aside to cool.

For the Persimmon Coulis

8 cups persimmon pulp	sugar to taste
2 cups water	cornstarch and water for thickening
1 tablespoon lemon zest	

PUREE the pulp with the water and zest, then simmer over medium low heat for twenty minutes. Add sugar to taste and thicken with a light cornstarch slurry. Set aside.

For the Tamarind Lacquer

4 cups orange juice	2 tablespoons tamarind
½ cup white wine	¼ cup soy sauce
1 cup reserved duck stock	1 cup brown sugar
2 tablespoons ginger, minced	

COMBINE all ingredients and simmer on medium high heat until reduced by a third. Strain and return to the heat in a clean saucepan. Reduce further and put through a chinois.

TAMARIND LACQUERED DUCKLING
with Persimmon Coulis and Cellophane Noodle Vegetable Slaw
CONTINUED

For the Ponzu Sauce (for the cellophane salad)

- ½ cup soy sauce
- ½ ounce sweet chili
- ½ ounce Sambal Olek
- 2 tablespoons sugar mixed with ½ cup hot water
- 1 teaspoon garlic, crushed
- ½ ounce fresh ginger
- 1 tablespoon sesame oil
- ¼ teaspoon Chinese five spice
- 1 tablespoon lime juice
- 2 green onions, minced

COMBINE all ingredients and let stand one hour.

For the Cellophane Noodle and Root Vegetable Slaw

- ½ pound cellophane noodles (hydrated in hot water)
- 1 golden beet
- 1 small carrot
- 1 small daikon radish
- 1 red pepper
- 2 ounces roasted peanuts
- 1 cucumber
- ¼ cup mint and cilantro, chiffonade

PREPARE ingredients. Julienne or use a vegetable curler to curl the beets, carrots, and radish. Peel seed and slice cucumber. Julienne peppers and chiffonade herbs. Set ingredients aside until assembling dish at serving time.

Serves 4

The Broadmoor

THE BROADMOOR
COLORADO SPRINGS

1 Lake Avenue
Colorado Springs,
CO 80906
(800) 634-7711
www.thebroadmoor.com

Charles Court
Dinner Tues-Sun
Penrose Room
Dinner Mon-Sat

The Broadmoor

The Grande Dame of the Rockies has been luxuriously hosting guests for over 85 years. Prior to the opening of the Broadmoor Main complex in June 1918, the land housed the Broadmoor Dairy Farm, established in 1880 by Willie Wilcox. The unsuccessful dairy farm was followed by an unsuccessful casino and hotel. The true birth of the Grand Dame was in May 1916, when Spencer Penrose, a Philadelphia entrepreneur who had made his fortune in gold and copper mining, purchased the 40-acre site of the casino and hotel, along with an adjoining 400 acres.

Penrose had a dream of turning the Pikes Peak region into a multi-faceted resort area. He hired a team of architects and designers who imported artisans from Italy and other European countries to create ornate moldings and paintings to adorn the interior as well as elaborate detailing on the Italian Renaissance exterior. A brilliant entrepreneur, Penrose also built the famous Pikes Peak Road to the summit. He also established the Cheyenne Mountain Zoo, and in 1925, he purchased and modernized the Pikes Peak Cog Railway. Penrose marketed The Broadmoor as the "European alternative", attracting many visitors to the resort for the clean mountain air that was said to relieve the symptoms of tuberculosis and other bronchial maladies.

Today, the same gracious and impeccable service that Penrose required of his staff is still in evidence. This is a perfect destination for a romantic getaway or a family vacation. The amenities include three championship golf courses, including nine holes built by Robert Trent Jones. Swimmers have a choice of three pools: an indoor pool, and outdoor lap pool, or the spectacular infinity edge swimming pool located at the north end of Cheyenne Lake. The Stables at The Broadmoor offer a unique western horseback riding experience, and the seven plexi-cushion tennis courts in the Broadmoor Tennis Complex will help you to work up an appetite for a fabulous meal in one of The Broadmoor's many restaurants.

Of the eleven restaurants on the resort's grounds, be sure to have at least one dinner in either the Penrose Room, located in the Broadmoor Main, or the Charles Court located in the Broadmoor West. With a wine cellar that contains over 3,000 bottles, both restaurants have consistently won the Best of Awards of Excellence from the Wine Spectator.

Best of Award of Excellence
Charles Court

Award of Excellence
Penrose Room

240

The Broadmoor, Colorado Springs

BUTTERNUT SQUASH AND APPLE BISQUE

Ingredients

1 *large butternut squash, peeled and diced*	2 *cups heavy cream*
½ *cup onion, diced*	1 *cup apple juice*
2 *tablespoons butter*	1 *teaspoon cinnamon*
½ *cup white wine*	½ *teaspoon nutmeg*
4 *cups chicken stock*	1 *apple, medium diced*

Preparation

SWEAT the onions in the butter. Add the butternut squash and sweat. Deglaze the pan with the white wine and reduce to ¼ cup of liquid. Add the chicken stock, heavy cream, and apple juice, and cook on medium heat until the squash is tender. Puree the mixture and season to taste with salt and pepper. Add the nutmeg and cinnamon. If the soup is too thick, add more stock. Add the diced apples as a garnish to finish.

Serves 8

Wine suggestion: Markham Sauvignon Blanc, Hess Select Chardonnay

SALMON FLORENTINE
with Quenelle of Sole en Croûte

Ingredients

7 ounces salmon filet	¼ teaspoon onion
¼ teaspoon shallots	4 ounces drawn butter
¼ ounce fresh lemon	3 ounces spinach
¼ ounce white wine	4 sheets phyllo dough
⅓ teaspoon garlic	Quenelle (recipe follows)

Preparation

PREHEAT oven to 350 degrees. Season the salmon filet with the shallot, lemon, and white wine. Set the salmon aside. Sauté the garlic and onions in the drawn butter. Add the spinach to the garlic and onions. Cook and then cool down. Lay down a single sheet of phyllo dough, brush it with the drawn butter. Put another sheet on top of the first and brush that with butter. Repeat until all dough is used. Place salmon filet in the center of the phyllo dough, top with spinach mixture and pull the dough together over the salmon. Bake for 8-12 minutes in 350 degree oven. Serve with poached quenelle.

For the Quenelle

6 ounces sole	2 tablespoons sherry
2½ tablespoons egg whites	pinch dill
1½ tablespoons heavy cream	salt and pepper to taste
1 slice bread	poaching liquid to cover

COMBINE all ingredients in a food processor or a blender. Form mixture into long tapered cylindrical shapes. Test a small portion in poaching liquid at 165 degrees.

Serves 1

Wine Suggestion: Cakebread Cellars Sauvignon Blanc or Chalk Hill Chardonnay

CHARLES COURT PEPPER STEAK

Ingredients

6 ounces center cut filet mignon
2 shallots, brunoise
3 teaspoons Dijon mustard
    pinch cracked green peppercorns
    pinch cracked black peppercorns
½ cup chutney

¼ cup brandy
½ cup demi-glace
¼ cup heavy cream
    salt to taste
½ fresh lemon

Preparation

SAUTÉ filet until desired doneness, and set aside. Add the shallots, mustard, peppercorns, and chutney to the hot sauté pan. Stir briskly and bring to a boil. Remove from heat and add brandy; ignite and burn off. When the flame has died down, add the demi-glace and bring to a boil. Add the cream and adjust the seasoning with salt and a few drops of lemon.

Serves 1

Wine suggestion: Kendall-Jackson "Grand Estates" Cabernet Sauvignon

CHEESECAKE BOMBE
with Chocolate Glaze

Ingredients

24 ounces cream cheese
⅔ cup sugar
4 eggs
2½ tablespoons Gran Marnier
    zest of 1 orange

12 ounces semi-sweet chocolate, chopped
½ cup milk
    seasonal berries or candied orange
    peel for garnish

Preparation

CREAM together cream cheese and sugar until smooth. Add in eggs, scraping the bowl. Add the Gran Marnier, orange zest and 1/3 of the semi-sweet chocolate, mix well until incorporated. Pour mixture into half round molds or coffee cups. Bake in a 325 degree oven until done, approximately 40 minutes. Unmold cheesecakes and place on a wire rack until cool.

FOR THE glaze, scald the milk, add remaining chopped chocolate, and stir until chocolate is completely melted. Pour the chocolate glaze over the cheesecakes to coat and refrigerate. To serve, garnish with seasonal berries, or candied orange peel.

8 servings

Beverage Suggestion: Champagne or Gran Marnier

Jake and Telly's
Greek Cuisine

JAKE

TELLY'S
GREEK CUISINE

2616 W. Colorado Ave.
Colorado Springs, CO 80904
719-633-0406
www.greekdining.com

May-September
Monday - Thursday
11:00 am – 10:00 pm
Friday and Saturday

11:00 am - 11:00 pm
Sunday 11:00 am – 9 pm
October-April
Monday - Thursday
11:00 am – 9:00 pm
Friday and Saturday
11:00 am - 10:00 pm
Sunday
11:00 am - 9:00 pm

Jake & Telly's Greek Cuisine

Jake and Telly Topakas, Owners

Jake and Telly's family have been in the restaurant business for over 50 years, starting back east in Philadelphia with their grandfather, father and uncle owning restaurants. The Topakas brothers moved to Colorado in 1997 and opened Jake & Telly's Greek Cuisine. Located in the old historical Colorado City in Colorado Springs, they have brought the only full service Greek restaurant to the area.

The restaurant, located on the second floor, is decorated in traditional Greek style with white walls and blue trim. Large windows in the main room look out onto the dining porch. The walls are decorated with paintings of Greek landscapes and Greek architecture.

The brothers' roots go back to the Greek island of Xios, in the Aegean Sea directly east from Athens. This is the island where their grandparents, Eleftherios and Maria Topakas were born. Most of the food prepared in their restaurant is taken from their grandmother's secret recipes. Along with some new and innovative dishes using Greek ingredients, Jake and Telly serve traditional Greek food, Old World style. You'll find traditional Mousaka, Pasticcio, Lamb Kivestsi, Souvlaki, Greek Pork Chops and newer entrees such as Chicken Karfa.

The brothers are as passionate about good wine as they are about good food. They have a wonderful selection of Greek wines as well as a variety of wines from all over the world.

They are happy to help you select a Greek wine to complement the dishes you select.

Between the luscious flavors of the Greek dishes, the Greek wine, the beautiful Greek landscape paintings, and especially the infectious hospitality of the staff, you will feel as if you had visited the Greek Islands yourself.

Y Award of Excellence

DOLMADES

Ingredients

1 cup uncooked rice
2 cups water
1 cup minced onion
½ cup minced garlic
½ cup extra virgin olive oil
1 pound ground beef
1 tablespoon salt
1 tablespoon pepper
12 ounce jar of grape leaves in water
4 cups heavy whipping cream

1 cup fresh lemon juice
½ cup chopped fresh basil
pinch of salt
pinch of pepper
lemon wheel (optional, for garnish)
chopped parsley
(optional, for garnish)
grilled pita bread wedges
(optional, for garnish)

Preparation

COOK white rice in a pot, 2 to 1 ratio, water to rice. When rice is finished, set off to the side. In new pot, sauté onion and garlic in olive oil until translucent, then add ground beef. When beef is cooked to a medium, add salt and pepper. When ground beef is finished add to white rice, mix thoroughly.

TO MAKE dolmades, take 2 large grape leaves, place on smooth surface stem to stem. Place spoonful of beef-rice mixture onto grape leaf and fold over sides and roll. When all dolmades are rolled, place firmly in 2-inch pan. Cover with water, then place a perforated 2-inch pan over top of dolmades and place two or three small plates on perforated pan to give it weight. Place dolmades on stove, on medium flame, boil for 20 minutes or until grape leaves are tender (one way of knowing when grape leaves are finished is that the leaves seem to have a gray, stained look).

FOR THE sauce, place a saucepan over medium flame, pour in heavy whipping cream, lemon juice, basil, pinch of salt, and a pinch of pepper. Cook until sauce is thickened, stirring often.

TO SERVE, stack three dolmades in a bowl, pour sauce over top, garnish with lemon wheel, chopped parsley, and grilled pita bread wedges.

Serves 4

Wine suggestion: 2002 Biblia Chora

ROAST LAMB SHANK

This entrée is one of our signature dishes. It's the most popular of all our entrees. It has been on our menu since we became a full Greek restaurant. The recipe has been handed down to Telly and I from our grandmother, who came from the island of Xios.

Ingredients

4 lamb hind shanks	½ cup fresh garlic, chopped
2 cups red wine	½ cup fresh onion, chopped
2 tablespoons salt	6 cups tomato puree
1 tablespoon black pepper	Orzo (recipe follows)

Preparation

PREHEAT oven to 400 degrees. Place lamb shanks in baking pan with 4-inch sides. Pour wine over shanks. Add seasoning lightly over all shanks. Sprinkle garlic and onion over shanks, and add puree over each shank. Cover with foil and roast in oven at 400 degrees for 5¼ hours. Sauce is complete when lamb shanks are finished.

TO SERVE, place orzo in large flat bowl, place shank, standing bone up, on orzo and finish with sauce.

For the Orzo

6½ cups water	1½ cups crumbled feta cheese
3 cups uncooked orzo	2 teaspoons salt
2 cups diced tomato	1 teaspoon black pepper

PLACE water in pot, bring to boil, add orzo. When orzo is cooked to your liking, strain and add tomato, feta, and seasoning. Mix well and serve.

Serves 4

Wine Pairing: 1999 Ktima Kir-Yianni Ramnista, Naoussa

MOUSAKAS

This dish is one of the most well known dishes throughout all of Greece. While everyone makes it, everyone makes it differently. This recipe was handed down to me from my grandmother from Xios. Although this dish can be made with lamb, it's more expensive with lamb, and mostly done with ground beef, though I think lamb was the original ingredient.

Ingredients

2   large eggplant, unpeeled
½   cup of salt (for sweating eggplant)
3   large potatoes, peeled
½   onion, chopped fine
½   cup of extra virgin olive oil
2½ pounds fresh ground beef or lamb
1½ cups tomato puree
1   tablespoon ground thyme
1   tablespoon ground sage
1   tablespoon dry basil
1   tablespoon dry oregano

1   tablespoon salt
1   teaspoon black pepper
    flour (for dusting eggplant slices)
    oil for frying and basting
2   cups Parmesan cheese, grated (if you
    can't find Kefalotiri)
½   pound butter
2   cups flour
½   gallon whole milk
3   eggs, beaten

Preparation

BEGIN with slicing eggplant in about 1-inch thick circular pieces. Lay eggplant over large baking sheet, and sprinkle with salt (this removes the bitterness from the eggplant). Peel potatoes, slice length-wise in 1-inch slices. Neatly place potato slices in a baking pan with four-inch sides, covering entire bottom surface of pan.

PRE-HEAT oven to 375 degrees, baste tops of potato with oil and place in oven, uncovered. Cook potatoes until lightly browned and cooked all the way through. While potatoes are cooking, place chopped onion and olive oil in a pot. Sauté onion until soft, then add ground beef. When ground beef is cooked, add the tomato puree, all of the seasoning, and mix well. Turn off heat on beef.

REMOVE eggplant from baking sheet, flour each piece of eggplant. Fry eggplant in vegetable oil, or oil of your liking, to golden brown, but not too crunchy. When eggplant is finished, begin the layering process. In the pan the potatoes are in, sprinkle a portion of the Parmesan cheese, then spread ground beef covering the potatoes entirely. Sprinkle more of the Parmesan cheese over the beef, then layer eggplant over the beef, covering the entire surface.

MOUSAKAS

CONTINUED

TO MAKE the sauce, melt butter in saucepan, add flour, and beat until roux is cooked. Slowly add milk, stirring constantly. When all milk is added, or sauce is to the consistency of your liking, add beaten eggs (I prefer it very thick, it holds better). Pour sauce over casserole and spread evenly, bake in oven at 375 degrees for one hour or until sauce is lightly browned. Remove from the oven, allow moussaka to set for 45 minutes to an hour. Then serve.

Serves 4

Wine suggestion: 2001 Skouras St. George Namea

Pike's Peak Avenue, Colorado Springs. (between 1908 and 1910)

FARMERS MARKETS

Farmer's Markets are popular throughout the United States. Since 1994, the number of Farmer's Markets has increased by 79 percent, to more than 3,000 nationwide.

While the sales at these venues currently account for about 2% of the total U.S. produce sales, it seems the public has discovered the joys and benefits of shopping Farmer's Markets and the word is spreading.

Fans cite the following for the upsurge in popularity: freshness, quality, price, and local access. People are also interested in organic foods and prefer to buy from the source. Organic producers favor direct marketing outlets, such as Farmer's Markets, and consumers like the chance to talk with the organic farmer personally.

Sometimes Farmer's Markets are the sole outlets for certain products. In a recent survey, 19,000 farmers reported selling exclusively at Farmer's Markets. The markets are accessible, low in cost, and flexible, and give producers a chance to answer questions and market directly. And Farmer's Markets are not limited to food products. Many of the open-air venues offer handcrafted items, unique artwork, jewelry, or the like.

Colorado and the Denver area have some outstanding Farmer's Markets. For example, the European marketplace atmosphere in Longmont is a delightful place to stroll. The tree-lined plaza features a selection of locally-grown vegetables and fruits, flowers, honey, artisan breads, farm-oriented crafts, bedding plants, farm fresh eggs, and more.

Most markets are open during the summer season, and specific information on location, directions, and hours can be found at www.coloradofarmersmarket.com, or phone 303-570-3276.

Agricultural Marketing Service has a Marketing Services Branch, which offers a web page on Farmer's Market activities, www.ams.usda.gov/farmersmarkets, or call the "Farmers Market Hotline" at 1-800-384-8704, for more information.

Whether you have an afternoon to kill or an ingredient list to fill, Farmer's Markets fit the bill.

CULINARY SOURCES

This list is only provided for your convenience. While many of the suggested suppliers have been recommended, not all suppliers have been individually checked out. We do not endorse any particular vendor or supplier.

FOOD

Bingham Hill
Blue cheese, livarot, sheep cheese, etc.
216 Commerce Drive Suite 6
Fort Collins, CO 80524
Phone: 970-472-0702
www.binghamhill.com

Broken Arrow Ranch
Venison and wild game
Phone: 1-800-962-4263
www.brokenarrowranch.com/

Coosemans-Denver, Inc.
Lollo rosso, mizun, specialty produce.
5135 Peoria Street
Denver, CO 80239
Phone: 303-371-3130
www.coosemansdenver.com/

Dean and Deluca
Duck Confit, fine foods, kitchenware, gifts, wine.
Phone: 877-826-9246
www.deandeluca.com

Diamond Organics
Mizuna, farm fresh organic food.
Highway 1
Moss Landing, CA 95039
Phone: 888-ORGANIC (674-2642)
www.diamondorganics.com

Finest Caviar
Wasabi tobiko and all kinds of caviar.
www.finest-caviar.com

Galloway's Naturally
Calymyrna figs, and specialty items.
9851 Van Horne Way
Richmond, British Columbia, Canada
Phone: 604-270-6363
www.gallowaysfoods.com

Game Sales International, Inc.
Wild game meats and specialty foods.
P.O. Box 7719
Loveland, CO 80537
Phone: 970-667-4090, 800-729-2090
www.gamesalesintl.com

Haystack Mountain
Award-winning farmstead goat cheese.
5239 Niwot Road
Niwot, Colorado 80503
Phone: 303-581-9948
www.haystackgoatcheese.com

igourmet
Manchego cheese, ricotta salata, specialty cheeses, fine foods, exquisite gifts.
1735 Front St.
Yorktown Heights, NY 10598
Phone: 877-igourmet (446-8763)
www.igourmet.com

Maple Leaf Farms – Duck
800-382-5546 / 800-348-2812
www.mapleleaffarms.com

Melissa's/World Variety Produce, Inc.
Galia melon, blood oranges, organic and exotic fruits and vegetables.
P.O. Box 21127
Los Angeles, CA 90021
800-588-0151
www.melissas.com

Napa Style Store
Tellicherry peppercorns, specialty items.
www.napastyle.com

Penzeys Spices
Juniper berries, spices from around the world.
Phone: 800-741-7787
www.penzeys.com

Red Bird Farms Co.
Red Bird Chicken
P.O. Box 1197
Englewood, CO 80150-1197
Phone: 303-934-2200
Toll Free: 800-333-BIRD (2473)
www.redbirdchicken.com

Rocky Mountain Shiitake
Shiitake mushrooms.
303-984-0119

Syracuse's Sausage
Linguisa sausage, Wisconsin-style bratwurst, chorizo, Andouille and other sausages.
903 N. Hwy 156
P.O. Box 118
Ponder, Texas 76259
Phone: 940-479-2700
Toll-Free: 800-525-8540
www.syracusesausage.com

Vallero Mercantile
Specialty Foods
3875 Steele Street Apt A
Denver, CO 80205
303-383-1606

COOKING SUPPLIES AND EQUIPMENT

Kitchen Collection
Silicone baking mats, kitchen accessories.
Phone: 888-548-2651
www.kitchencollection.com

Kitchen Emporium
Blini pan, kitchen accessories.
888-858-7920
www.kitchenemporium.com

Peppercorn
Gourmet kitchen store.
1235 Pearl St.
Denver, CO 80302
303-449-5847
800-442-6905
www.peppercorn.com

Sur La Table
Gourmet kitchen store.
1-800-243-0852
www.surlatable.com

WINE AND SPIRITS

Clear Creek Distillery
Williams Pear, American Calvados Apple, and other fine fruit brandies
1430 Northwest 23rd
Portland, OR. 97210
Phone: 503-248-9470
www.clearcreekdistillery.com

Ficklin Vineyards
Ficklin port
30246 Avenue 7½
Madera, CA 93637
Phone: 559-674-4598
www.ficklin.com

GLOSSARY

al dente Italian for "to the tooth," describing pasta or other food cooked only until it offers a slight resistance when bitten into, but which is not soft or overdone.

arepas A round, maize-based bread popular in Venezuela. Arepas are often filled with meats or cheese, sometimes even fruit or vegetables.

Asiago cheese A semifirm Italian cheese with a rich, nutty flavor, made from whole or part-skim cow's milk.

bain-marie A term indicating a container placed inside another container of water so the food cooks gently.

beurre blanc "White butter," this sauce is composed of wine, vinegar, shallots, and butter.

blanch Plunging food (usually vegetables and fruits) into boiling water briefly, then into cold water to stop the cooking process.

Bosc pear A large winter pear with a sweet-tart flavor, this pear holds its shape when baked or poached.

braise Browning food (usually meat or vegetables) first in fat, then cooking in a small amount of liquid, covered, at low heat for a long time.

brunoise A mixture of vegetables that have been finely diced or shredded, then cooked slowly in butter.

Calvados A dry apple brandy from Calvados, the Normandy region of northern France, often used in dishes with chicken, pork and veal.

capers The flower bud of a bush native to the Mediterranean and parts of Asia, picked, sun-dried, and then pickled.

carpaccio Usually served as an appetizer, this Italian creation has thin shavings of raw beef fillet, drizzled with olive oil and lemon juice or served with a mayonnaise or mustard sauce, and garnished with capers or onions.

caul A thin, fatty membrane resembling a lacy net, the caul lines the abdominal cavity. It's usually obtained from pigs or sheep and is used to wrap dishes like crépinettes, where it melts during the baking or cooking process.

Châteaubriand Châteaubriand is a type of recipe using a succulent, thick cut of beef (usually taken from the center of the tenderloin) that's large enough for two people.

chèvre cheese French for "goat," chèvre is a pure white goat's-milk cheese with a tart flavor.

chiffonade Similar to julienne, the process of cutting lettuce, endive, or herbs into thin, even strips.

chinois A very fine mesh cone-shaped metal sieve used for pureeing or straining. Often a spoon or pestle is used to press the food through it.

chipotle A dried, smoked, jalapeno with a sweet, almost chocolaty flavor.

cioppino This fish stew, usually with a tomato base, includes a variety of fish and shellfish. The dish was originated by Italian immigrants in San Francisco.

clarified	The process of clearing a cloudy substance, such as in stocks or wines, or melting butter until the foam rises and is skimmed off.
concassé	A coarsely chopped mixture, often made up of tomatoes.
confit	A French word from a term meaning "to prepare," used for meat that has been cooked and preserved in its own fat.
conserve	A thick mixture of fruits, nuts and sugar, cooked together and often used on biscuits, or as garnish.
coulis	A general term meaning a thick puree or sauce.
court bullion	A poaching liquid usually made up of vegetables, water, herbs and wine or vinegar.
crème anglaise	A custard sauce with cream, sugar, egg yolks, and, usually, vanilla for flavoring.
crème fraîche	A thick, velvety cream that can be boiled without curdling.
crépinette	A small, slightly flattened sausage is made of minced pork, lamb, veal or chicken, sometimes with truffles. Crépinettes are usually cooked by coating them in melted butter and breadcrumbs before sautéing, grilling, or broiling.
curry powder	Popular in Indian cooking, curry powder is a mixture of as many as 20 spices, herbs, and seeds. It comes in two basic styles — standard, and the hotter of the two, "Madras."
daikon	A large Asian radish with a sweet, fresh flavor.
deglaze	Adding wine or water to the skillet to loosen browned bits on the bottom to make a sauce.
demi-glace	A rich brown sauce (usually meat stock) combined with Madeira or sherry and slowly cooked until it's reduced by half to a thick glaze.
demi-sec	In cooking, it refers to reducing by half. In wine, it refers to the level of sweetness.
devein	Taking out the gray-black intestinal vein from the back of a shrimp.
duxelles	A garnish or flavoring made of finely chopped sautéed mushrooms, shallots, and herbs.
fermented black beans	Fermented black beans are small, black soybeans preserved in salt. Sometimes called Chinese black beans or salted black beans, the beans have a strong, salty flavor and are usually soaked for a half hour or so in fresh water before being added to a dish.
fines herbes	A combination of very finely chopped herbs, traditionally chervil, chives, parsley, and tarragon, used in cooking.
focaccia	Italian bread with a large, flat round shape, brushed or drizzled with olive oil and sprinkled with salt.
foie gras	The term generally used for goose liver.
french, to	To trim fat or bone from a cut of meat.

Galia melons	Galias, a hybrid cross between honeydew and cantaloupe, have green flesh and sweet taste.
grappa	A colorless, high alcohol Italian spirit distilled from the grape skins and seeds remaining in the wine press after the wine has been made.
gremolata	This garnish is made of minced parsley, citrus zest, garlic, oil, and salt, and it's often sprinkled over osso buco for a fresh accent.
hoisin	A sauce of soybeans, garlic, chili peppers and various spices used in Chinese cooking.
julienne	A method of cutting vegetables into thin strips, usually about 1 inch by 1/16 inch.
kosher salt	An additive-free coarse-grained salt.
lollo rosso, lolo rosa, lolla rossa	There are many different spelling for this ruffled leaf lettuce, which has a distinctive red coloration. It has a light crunchy texture and is often an ingredient in mesclun.
Manchego cheese	Cheese from the La Mancha region of Spain, made from raw sheep's milk. The flavor is zesty and the texture is firm and tends to be dry.
mesclun	A mix of young, small salad greens, such as arugula, dandelion and radicchio.
mirepoix; mirepois	A mixture of diced carrots, onions, celery, and herbs sautéed in butter.
mirin	A sweet, rice wine used in cooking to sweeten meat or fish dishes.
mise en place	To have all the ingredients necessary for a dish and be ready to combine for cooking.
mizuna	Green leaf mustard green with saw-toothed leaves. Often found in mesclun, mizuna has a mild, tangy flavor. Also called Xiu Cai, Kyona, Japanese Mustard, Potherb Mustard, Japanese Greens or California Peppergrass.
mole	Mole is a smooth, cooked blend of onion, garlic, chilies, ground pumpkin, or sesame seeds, and a small amount of Mexican chocolate, its best-known ingredient.
mount, to	A cooking technique where small, cold, unsalted butter chunks are whisked into a sauce right before it's served.
mousseline	A sauce, such as hollandaise, with whipped cream, crème fraîche, or beaten egg whites added.
osso buco	Veal shanks cooked slowly in olive oil, white wine, stock, onions, tomatoes, garlic, anchovies, carrots, celery and lemon peel.
paella	A Spanish rice dish with meats, shellfish, or vegetables, usually flavored with saffron.
panko	Coarse bread crumbs (Japanese) used for coating fried foods.
phyllo	Thin layers of pastry dough used in sweet and savory recipes.
poaching	Cooking by submerging an item in a liquid that is just barely simmering.

ponzu sauce	A Japanese sauce made with lemon juice or rice vinegar, mirin and/or sake, kombu and dried bonito flakes often used as a dipping sauce.
prosciutto	Italian word for ham; seasoned, salt-cured and air-dried, but not smoked.
purée	To grind or mash food until it's completely smooth, using a food processor, a blender, or by forcing the food through a sieve.
quenelle	A light dumpling made of minced or ground fish, meat or vegetables seasoned, and bound with eggs. This mixture is formed into small ovals and gently poached in stock.
queso blanco	A white, mild, fresh Mexican cheese with a firm texture. Queso blanco is sometimes called queso fresco.
ramekin	An individual earthenware-baking dish similar to a miniature soufflé dish.
rapini	Another name for broccoli raab, a leafy green vegetable with 6- to 9-inch stalks and scattered clusters of tiny broccoli-like buds. Rapini is popular in many Italian dishes.
reduce, reduction	To boil a liquid rapidly, reducing it until it's thickened and flavorful.
render	To convert or melt down fat by slow heating.
rice paper	An edible, translucent paper made from water combined with the rice-paper plant, an Asian shrub, and used to wrap foods. Rice paper can be found in Asian markets and some supermarkets.
ricotta salata	A smooth, firm sheep's milk Italian cheese, lightly salted. In a pinch, feta cheese can be substituted, if it's soaked for an hour in cold water prior to use.
rillette	Meat slowly cooked in seasoned fat, then pounded or pulverized into a paste.
roux	A mixture of equal parts flour and butter used to thicken sauces. Cooking different lengths of time results in different flavors and colors.
Sambal Oelek	Chilies with no additives such as garlic or spices, it can be used to add heat to a dish without altering the other delicate flavors. Available in Asian markets.
sauté	To quickly cook food over direct heat in a small amount of hot oil.
sauterne	A full-bodied sweet white wine from the Bordeaux region of France.
sec	This French word means "dry".
semifreddo	An Italian word, meaning "half cold," this refers to a chilled or partially frozen dessert.
shallot	Member of the onion family, with a flavor of a combination of garlic and onion.
streusel	A crumb-like topping.
strudel	A pastry, rolled up in a thin sheet of dough and baked.
sweat	To cook vegetables slowly in a tightly covered pan so that they literally stew in their own juice.
Tabasco pepper; Tabasco Sauce	A small, hot, red pepper originally from the Mexican state of Tabasco. The word, meaning "damp earth," is trademarked by the McIlhenny family.

tamarind	The tamarind is the fruit of a tall shade tree found in Asia, northern Africa, and India. The long pods have a sour-sweet pulp that is popular as a flavoring in East Indian and Middle Eastern cuisines.
tapenade	A spread or condiment, usually consisting of puréed capers, olives, and anchovies in olive oil.
temper	To warm beaten eggs, by stirring a little of the hot ingredients into them, before adding the hot ingredients in entirety, so the eggs don't solidify.
truffle	A fungus that is cultivated primarily in France and Italy, valued for its earthy, aromatic nature.
truffle oil	Truffle oil is created when truffles are soaked in olive oil.
turbinado sugar	Raw sugar that has been steam-cleaned. The coarse turbinado crystals are blond colored and have a delicate molasses flavor.
wasabi	Sometimes called Japanese horseradish, this green-colored condiment comes in paste and powder form.
water bath	A term indicating a container placed inside another container of water so the food cooks gently.
wilted spinach/lettuce	Wilting spinach or lettuce, by steaming or drizzling hot liquid over them.
Zabaglione	A custard-like dessert made by whisking together egg yolks, wine and sugar.
zest	The brightly colored outermost skin layer of citrus fruit, removed with a zester, grater, or knife.

ABOUT THE PUBLISHERS

Chuck and Blanche Johnson started Wilderness Adventures Press, Inc. in 1993, publishing outdoor and sporting books. Along with hunting and fishing, they love fine dining, good wines, and traveling. They have always been able to "sniff out" the most outstanding and interesting restaurants in any city they visit.

On weekends, they experiment in the kitchen, cooking a variety of fish and meats, as well as preparing the harvest from their time in the field. This love of cooking has resulted in a large library of cookbooks, and has inspired them to create a series of cookbooks based on their love of travel and fine dining.

Chuck and Blanche make their home in Gallatin Gateway, Montana, along with their four German wirehaired pointers.

Photo Copyrights/Credits

Cover, left to right across: ©Nico's Catacombs; ©Denver Public Library; ©Buckhorn Exchange; ©Brasserie Rouge; ©The Broadmoor; ©The Fort; ©Red Lion; ©Tracy Johnson; ©Clipart.com; ©The Fort; ©Denver Public Library; ©The Fort. **Back cover, left to right across:** ©Tracy Johnson; ©Restaurant Kevin Taylor; ©Jay's Bistro; ©Tracy Johnson; ©Tracy Johnson; ©The Cliff House.

All photos ©Tracy Johnson unless noted. **i:** Denver Public Library, Western History Collection, Wm. Henry Jackson, WHJ-755. **viii-large:** ©Denver Public Library, Western History Collection, Harry M. Rhoads, Rh-668. **viii-small:** ©Colorado Historical Society. **x-large:** ©Denver Public Library, Western History Collection, L.C. McClure, MCC-1755. **x-small:** ©Denver Public Library, Western History Collection, Sanborn, X-29653. **2, 5:** ©1515 Restaurant. **16:** ©Barolo Grill. **20:** ©Denver Public Library, Western History Collection, L.C. McClure, MCC-835. **21, 22, 26, 28:** ©Brasserie Rouge. **29, 30, 34:** ©Buckhorn Exchange. **35, 36, 38:** ©Celtic Tavern. **42:** ©Denver Public Library, Western History Collection, X-23463. **50:** ©Denver Public Library, Western History Collection, L.C. McClure, MCC-1231. **52-bottom:** ©Painted Bench. **60, 62,63:** ©Aix Restaurant. **74-bottom, 76, 77:** ©Rocky Mountain Diner. **78:** ©Denver Public Library, Western History Collection, Z-3101. **86:** ©Denver Public Library, Western History Collection, X-29650. **88, 92:** ©Strings. **94, 96:** ©Fourth Story. **102:** The Fort. **109, 110, 112:** ©Chef Jam. **122:** ©Denver Public Library, Western History Collection, George Beam, GB-7128. **136:** Denver Public Library, Western History Collection, L.C.McClure, MCC-1756. **138:** ©Restaurant Kody. **147, 148:** ©Gabriel's. **152:** ©Denver Public Library, Western History Collection, Donald Kemp, K-160. **158:** ©Denver Public Library, Western History Collection, X-11655. **159, 160, 165-right, 166:** ©Flagstaff House. **168:** ©Greenbriar Inn. **177, 178, 180, 183:** ©Red Lion. **185, 186, 188, 190:** ©Savoy. **194:** ©Denver Public Library, Western History Collection, Miller, X-11009. **202, 26:** ©Jay's Bistro. **208, 211:** ©Nico's Catacombs. **214:** ©Black Bear Restaurant. **220:** ©Denver Public Library, Western History Collection, John Anderson, X-14733. **222:** ©Briarhurst Manor. **232:** ©The Cliff House. **240:** ©The Broadmoor. **246-bottom:** ©Jake & telly's Greek Cuisine. **250:** ©Denver Public Library, Western History Collection, L.C. McClure, MCC-1230. **254:** ©Colorado Historical Society.

INDEX

NOTES

NOTES

NOTES